Contemporary Irish Writers

Contemporary Irish Writers and Filmmakers

General Series Editor:

Eugene O'Brien, Head of English Department, Mary Immaculate College, University of Limerick.

Titles in the series:

Forthcoming:

Contemporary Irish Writers

John McGahern
From the Local to the Universal

Eamon Maher

The Liffey Press

Published by The Liffey Press
Ashbrook House, 10 Main Street,
Raheny, Dublin 5, Ireland.
www.theliffeypress.com

A catalogue record of this book is
available from the British Library.

ISBN 1-904148-40-9

*This book has been published with the assistance of grant-aid from
An Chomhairle Ealaíon, The Arts Council of Ireland*

Printed in the Republic of Ireland by ColourBooks Ltd.

Contents

About the Author

Eamon Maher is a Lecturer in Humanities at the Institute of Technology, Tallaght, in Dublin. His first book was a comparative study of twentieth-century Irish and French novelists, *Crosscurrents and Confluences: Echoes of Religion in 20th Century Fiction* (2000), and he was the recipient of the translation bursary, the *Prix de l'Ambassade*, for his translation of the memoir of the French novelist, Jean Sulivan, *Anticipate Every Goodbye* (2000). More recently he co-edited, with Michael Böss, the proceedings of the 2001 EFACIS (European Federation of Associations and Centres of Irish Studies) conference, *Engaging Modernity: Readings of Irish Politics, Literature and Culture at the Turn of the Century* (2003). He is currently working on a second book on John McGahern for a US publisher entitled *The Life and Works of John McGahern* as well as co-editing with Grace Neville the proceedings of a Franco-Irish conference held in IT Tallaght in March 2003: *France and Ireland: Anatomy of a Relationship* (Peter Lang). He has published widely on various aspects of the twentieth-century Irish and French novel in journals in Ireland, Great Britain and France.

Series Introduction

Given the amount of study that the topic of Irish writing, and increasingly Irish film, has generated, perhaps the first task of a series entitled *Contemporary Irish Writers and Filmmakers* is to justify its existence in a time of diminishing rainforests. As Declan Kiberd's *Irish Classics* has shown, Ireland has produced a great variety of writers who have influenced indigenous, and indeed, world culture, and there are innumerable books devoted to the study of the works of Yeats, Joyce and Beckett. These writers spoke out of a particular Irish culture, and also transcended that culture to speak to the Anglophone world, and beyond.

However, Ireland is now a very different place from that which figures in the works of Yeats, Joyce and Beckett, and it seems timely that the representations of this more secular, more European, and more cosmopolitan Ireland should be investigated and it is with this in mind that *Contemporary Irish Writers and Filmmakers* has been launched.

This series will examine the work of writers and filmmakers who have engaged with the contemporary cultural issues that are important in Ireland today. Irish literature and film has often been viewed as obsessed with the past, but contemporary writers and filmmakers seem to be involved in a process of negotiation between the Ireland of the past and the Ireland of the coming times. It is on this process of negotiation that much of our current imaginative literature and film is focused, and this series hopes to investigate this process through the chosen *auteurs*.

Indeed, it is a sign of the maturity of these *auteurs* that many of them base their narratives not only in the setting of this "new Ireland", but often beyond these shores. Writers and filmmakers such as Seamus Heaney, John Banville, William Trevor and Neil Jordan have the confidence to write and work as *artists* without the necessary addendum of the qualifying "Irish". Their concerns, themes and settings take them outside Ireland to a global stage. Yet, as this series attests, their "Irishness", however that is defined, remains intact and is often imprinted even in their most "international" works.

Politically and culturally, contemporary Ireland is in something of a values deficit as the previous hegemonic certainties of party political and religious allegiance have been lost in a plethora of scandals involving church and state. The role of art and culture in redefining the value-ethic for our culture has never been more important, and these studies will focus on the notions of Irishness and identity that prevail in the late twentieth and early twenty-first centuries.

The role of the aesthetic in the shaping of attitudes and opinions cannot be understated and these books will attempt to understand the transformative potential of the work of the artist in the context of the ongoing redefinition of society and culture. The current proliferation of writers and filmmakers of the highest quality can be taken as an index of the growing confidence of this society, and of the desire to enunciate that confidence. However, as Luke Gibbons has put it: "a people has not found its voice until it has expressed itself, not only in a body of creative works, but also in a body of critical works", and *Contemporary Irish Writers and Filmmakers* is part of such an attempt to find that voice.

Aimed at the student and general reader alike, it is hoped that the series will play its part in enabling our continuing participation in the great humanistic project of understanding ourselves and others.

Eugene O'Brien
Department of English
Mary Immaculate College
University of Limerick

Acknowledgements

I wish to thank my father, Liam, for his painstaking reading of the manuscript and his invaluable editorial advice.

The Institute of Technology, Tallaght awarded me a generous grant from its Seed Fund to help me to devote time to writing this book. The library staff there also gave me much support in acquiring the books and articles that I needed.

Eugene O'Brien, the editor of this series, provided me with the opportunity of being part of a great initiative and is a friend and editor whose judgement I trust completely. Brian Langan of the Liffey Press also offered vital suggestions that have improved the overall quality of the book.

John McGahern is unspoilt by his success and standing in the literary world and has shown me much kindness and openness in the past few years. I am especially indebted to him for the interview which appears at the end of this study.

Declan Kiberd supplied me with encouragement when I was at the early stages of writing this book and also did an informative and insightful interview with me on the work of John McGahern.

My wife and children are all hugely supportive of my literary endeavours and the book is rightfully dedicated to them.

To Liz, Liam, Marcella and Kevin

Chronology

1934	John McGahern born in Dublin on 12 November, one of seven children born to a Garda Sergeant and a national school teacher. In the early years, children live with mother in different parts of Leitrim (Ballinamore, Aughavas, Aughawilliam) while father works in Cootehall (County Roscommon).
1944	Death of mother; moves to live with father in the barracks in Cootehall. Attends the Presentation Brothers' secondary school in Carrick-on-Shannon. Gets access to library of local Protestant family, the Moroneys, and begins to read various authors: Zane Grey, Dickens, etc.
1954	After gaining a scholarship to Saint Patrick's Teacher Training College, graduates and begins teaching career in Drogheda (County Louth). Also studies in University College Dublin for BA.
1955	Moves to Dublin to take up a position as teacher in Scoil Eoin Baiste (Clontarf). Beginning of literary vocation — frequents some of the Dublin literary circles. Meets Patrick Kavanagh on a few occasions as well as other well-known literary figures.

1957	Conferred with BA from University College, Dublin. Begins work on (unpublished) first novel entitled *The End and the Beginning of Love.*
1961	In April of this year, produces an abbreviated form of novel, "The End and the Beginning of Love", which is published in *X: A Literary Magazine.*
1962	First literary prize, the AE Memorial Award of the Irish Arts Council, for abstract from first novel, *The Barracks.*
1963	In February, *The Barracks* is published to critical acclaim.
1964	McGahern is the recipient of the Macauley Fellowship which allows him to avail of a one-year sabbatical from teaching duties in Scoil Eoin Baiste. Spends the year abroad, mostly in England.
1965	Gets married to a Finn, the theatre director and translator, Annikki Laaksi. In May, *The Dark* is published and banned by the Irish Censorship of Publications and Films Board. Returns to Ireland and is fired from his teaching position in Scoil Eoin Baiste by the school manager, Fr Carton. Moves to London where he works on the buildings and as a supply teacher.
1968	Becomes Research Fellow at the University of Reading and recommences writing fiction.
1969	Appointed visiting Professor, Colgate University, New York for the first time (spends a semester there).
1970	Publication of *Nightlines.* Moves back to live in Ireland with Madeline Green. After spending sometime in Connemara, they buy a small farm in County Leitrim, where they still live.
1972	Visiting Professor, Colgate University (four months).
1973	Marriage to Madeline Green.

1974	Publication of *The Leavetaking*. Recipient of Society of Authors Travelling Scholarship.
1976	Visiting Professor, Colgate University.
1977	Writer-in-residence in University College Dublin (three months).
1978	Publication of *Getting Through*.
1978–79	Visiting Professor, Colgate University (one year).
1979	Publication of *The Pornographer*.
1983–84	Visiting Professor, Colgate University (one year).
1984	Revised edition of *The Leavetaking* published.
1985	Publication of *High Ground*. Recipient of the Irish American Foundation Award.
1986	*The Rockingham Shoot* is filmed and shown on BBC television.
1987	Visiting Professor of Creative Writing for two months at the University of Victoria (Canada).
1988	Begins a semester as Writer-in-Residence at Trinity College, Dublin.
1989	Awarded the *Chevalier des Arts et Lettres* by the President of France.
1990	Publication of *Amongst Women*. Shortlisted for the Booker Prize. Wins the *Irish Times*/Aer Lingus Irish Fiction Prize as well as *The Sunday Independent*/Irish Life Arts Award and the Bank of Ireland and Hughes Award.
1991	Honorary Doctorate awarded by Trinity College, Dublin. Visiting Professor at Colgate (four months). Publication of first play, *The Power of Darkness*, which is staged at the Abbey Theatre.
1992	Honorary Doctorate, University College Galway.

1993	Publication of the *Collected Stories*.
1996	Writer-in-residence, University College Dublin (three months). Awarded *Prix Étranger Écureuil*.
1997	Honorary Doctorate, Université de Poitiers.
1998	*Amongst Women* adapted for a BBC/RTÉ television drama. Wins a number of awards.
2000	Publication of *Selected Letters of John Butler Yeats* (Jose Corti and Faber) with an Introduction by McGahern.
2002	Publication of *That They May Face the Rising Sun* in January. Published by Knopf in the US under the title, *By the Lake*. Honorary Doctorate, Dublin Institute of Technology. *That They May Face the Rising Sun* wins the Kerry Ingredients Fiction Prize, *The Sunday Independent/* Hughes and Hughes Novel of the Year award. Short-listed for the South Bank Show awards and for the IMPAC International Prize. Recipient of PEN Award for Lifetime Achievement. Introduction to John Williams's *Stoner* and *Augustus* for Vintage Classics.
2003	Introduction to a book of selected articles from Dick Walsh's political columns. Appointed to the Arts Council by Minister John O'Donoghue.

List of Abbreviations

B   *The Barracks*
D   *The Dark*
L   *The Leavetaking* (second edition, 1984)
P   *The Pornographer*
AW   *Amongst Women*
CS   *The Collected Stories*
RS   *That They May Face the Rising Sun*

Introduction

John McGahern has been a major force in Irish literature for the past few decades. When Declan Kiberd refers to you as "the foremost prose writer in English now in Ireland" (Maher and Kiberd, 2002: 86), it is a sign that you have left your mark in a significant way on the literary landscape. It is not a position that McGahern has attained easily. We all know the extent to which the banning of his second novel, *The Dark*, changed his life. He admitted to feeling "shame" (Maher, 2001: 79) and dismay at the controversy the incident evoked. Losing his job as a primary school teacher was the first outcome of the banning. This forced him to go into exile in England for a number of years, before being named visiting Professor at Colgate University in New York in 1969. He bought a small farm in Leitrim in 1970 and came back to live there in 1974.

The treatment meted out to him could easily have led to bitterness towards the Catholic Church (especially in light of the prominent role Archbishop John Charles McQuaid played in his dismissal) and towards the repressive attitudes that prevailed in Ireland during the 1950s. In spite of all the pain, he notes, somewhat paradoxically, that he has "nothing but gratitude to the (Catholic) Church" (Maher, 2001: 73). This is in stark contrast to the reaction of other writers, most notably Frank McCourt, to what they perceived as the unhealthy influence of religion on their lives. Thus we have the famous opening lines of *Angela's Ashes*:

> It was, of course, a miserable childhood: the happy childhood is hardly worth your while. Worse than the ordinary miserable childhood is the miserable Irish childhood, and worse yet is the miserable Irish Catholic childhood. (McCourt, 1999: 1)

McCourt is the author of just one of the many memoirs written by Irish people in the past decade that decry a miserable childhood and are critical of the negative influence of Catholicism on their lives. Compare that view with the opinion of McGahern:

> The Church was my first book and I would think it is still my most important book. At that time, there were very few books in the house. The only pictures we could see were religious pictures, the Stations of the Cross. The only music we would hear was religious hymns; and it's (*the Church*) all I came to know of ceremony, even of luxury — the tulips that used to come in the flat boxes when I was an altar boy, the candles, the incense. (Maher, 2001: 72)

John McGahern is not the type of man who views the past through tinted glasses. He remembers all too well the hardship of growing up in Roscommon, the death of his mother when he was only ten years old, his distant relationship with his father. He is not a writer who engages in either diatribe or didacticism. When we read his books and short stories, we are transported back in time to a rural Ireland that is very close to extinction, an Ireland where people worked the land in a way that moulded their character. They were hard, sometimes cruel people. They were also kind, neighbourly, and had a sense of honour that is rare today. Most readers can relate to the domineering father figure, the man who demands obedience, even worship, from his children — Moran in *Amongst Women* is a prototype in this regard. The young male and female characters who are finding their way in life, breaking away with difficulty from the family unit, are also easy to identify with. Nature — with her trees whose leaves produce sounds that speak intimately to our souls, with her animals, lakes, sea, land — is a major character in most of McGahern's writings. He writes about the things and the people that he knows best.

His books should be seen as part of a work in progress. Many of the same themes and settings recur but are dealt with in a different and a progressively more effective way. He chisels away at his work in an attempt to get his words right and his painstaking efforts produce a style that is deceptively simple and clear. By that I mean that there is a lot of complexity in what is, at first sight, very uncomplicated and down-to-earth prose. It is a question of finding the exact adjective or noun to capture a mood swing. The raising of an eyebrow or the swinging of an axe, the stinking sweatband of a hat, a smile that lights up everything around it, can all have significant reverberations. McGahern is masterful at describing situations and people in an economical style that never wastes its time trying to show off. If he is easy to read, it is precisely because he puts so much care into his writing. He has thought long and hard about what he is seeking to achieve from his art. At the centre of all his endeavours is the image:

> When I reflect on the image two things from which it cannot be separated come: the rhythm and the vision. The vision, that still and private world which each of us possesses and which others cannot see, is brought ̣life in rhythm. (McGahern, 1991d: 12)

̣to say that "art is an attempt to create a world in ̣e can live" but that this world is never permanent and ̣ust always be sought anew. McGahern's particular vision is one that lends itself to a lucid style that resonates in an authentic manner with its readers. It contains in its rhythm a tension that is the hallmark of all good art. It seeks a perfection that can never be achieved but which must nevertheless be sought after constantly by the artist: "rejecting, altering, shaping, straining towards the one image that will never come, the image on which our whole life took its most complete expression once" (McGahern, 1991d: 12). It is clear that he is embarked on a type of odyssey or quest that has religious overtones. (He is close to Joyce in this regard.) As we progress through McGahern's *oeuvre*, I will be attempting to point out how the style evolves and improves until it attains in the later works a limpidity and a transparency which illustrate that he has at least caught an outline of the artist's grail of perfection.

I entitled this book *From the Local to the Universal* because I feel that it encapsulates the essence of what McGahern sets out to achieve. He said once: "I think that all good writing is local, and by local I don't differentiate between Ballyfermot and north Roscommon. If the writer gets his words right, he'll make that local scene universal" (Maher, 2001: 81). He manages to meet his own challenge in his fictional writings and this is the source of their fascination and appeal in Ireland and abroad. He is an admirer of Tomás Ó Criomhthain's *An tOileánach* because of its style, which is, in his view, "a persistent way of seeing" (McGahern, 1987: 7). He marvels at the manner in which Ó Criomhthain manages to suppress his emotions and to reduce everything to its bare essentials: "So free is all the action of everything but what is essential that it could as easily have taken place on the shores of Brittany and Greece as on the Dingle Peninsula" (McGahern, 1987: 7). The same could be said of McGahern's own fictional universe. By delving into the enclosed lives of the inhabitants of rural Ireland, he manages to capture the key ingredients of what makes them what they are. Everything is a circle for them: "the road away becomes the road back" (*B*, 158). Their geographical displacements may separate his characters physically from their place of birth, but the roots are deep, the influences constant. The characters are, in a sense, their environment, be it familial, social or physical. (I don't mean to imply by this that McGahern is a naturalist, but he definitely does lend a good deal of weight to the importance of heredity and environment.)

McGahern is attempting to build up a picture of a civilisation that will soon have disappeared, that of the rural Ireland of his youth. He wants us to be able to commune with the practices, speech, joys and sorrows of the people with whom he grew up so that there might be a chronicle available for the generations to come. We will see this to be particularly true of his two most recent novels, *Amongst Women* and *That They May Face the Rising Sun*.

It should thus come as no surprise that Ó Criomhthain's literary undertaking appeals so much to McGahern who, in his own way, is trying to achieve a similar objective. Towards the end of his essay on Ó Criomhthain's book, McGahern points out the main quality that makes for the enduring quality of *An tOileánach*: "Unwittingly, through this island frame, we have been introduced into a complete representation of existence" (McGahern, 1987: 7). If we replace the setting of rural Ireland for the island frame, we have a good summary of McGahern's own literary achievement.

People should not make the mistake of thinking that capturing the local accurately is a simple task. It requires both distance and intimacy, detachment and engagement. As I have already stated, the material dealt with, as well as the settings in which they are acted out, are the same from *The Barracks* through to *That They May Face the Rising Sun*. We are placed in the west midlands of Ireland for the vast bulk of the novels and the short stories. Some characters recur in slightly different guises in several accounts.

This repetition in no way detracts from our enjoyment of the narrative. Readers feel at home with the setting and with the characters presented. They are comfortable in the knowledge that the narrative is going to dramatise a way of life that is familiar and yet which seems very remote from the Ireland of the beginning of the third millennium. There is an almost exotic atmosphere surrounding the characters as they recite the rosary, save the hay, feed the animals, struggle to make ends meet. One gets the impression that this universe represents a vital part of Ireland's cultural and social heritage. Denis Sampson captures it well:

> In fact, if we take all his novels and stories as a whole, and reassign the parts into a chronological sequence, there is no better record of the inner and outer stresses to which a rural Irish family was subject over a period of more than two generations. While McGahern has seemed to concentrate only on personal and do-mestic concerns, he has cunningly and obliquely been the Balzac of Roscommon-Leitrim, following the evolu-tion of a community through the focus of one family, al-though the name sometimes varies. (Sampson, 1991a: 5)

I would argue that such a feat is a very worthy accomplishment by any writer. As the loveable Jamesie says in *That They May Face the Rising Sun*: "I may not have travelled far but I know the whole world" (*RS*, 296). In this, he is close to the opinion voiced by McGahern: "I would think that I write out of my own private or spiritual world. I would see my business as to get my words right and I think that if you get your words right you will reflect everything that the particular form you're writ-ing in is capable of reflecting. . . . Art is a mysterious thing, the fingerprints of the writer are all over it and you can't fake any-thing from the reader. If the tension's not there, the reader will sense that it's actually not dramatised, not thought out, not felt" (Maher, 2001: 77). This is the reason why he doesn't buy into the paradigm of the Irish writer having to go into exile to nurture his art. In his view, you can write as badly in Ireland as abroad! In his present abode by a lake in Leitrim (a setting that closely resembles that of *That They May Face the Rising Sun*) McGahern has all the raw material he needs for his writing. John B. Keane always maintained that the street below his window in Listowel provided him with the characters, situations and inspiration for his plays.

The important thing, as pointed out by McGahern above, is to maintain the tension and not to fall into the trap of propaganda or journalism. It's not the role of the artist to set out to give a particular view of his country or its people. He must go where the characters and his interior voice lead him. He has admitted that the ideas with which he began many of his novels and stories were often pushed out by some other image or character. In an interview with Mike Murphy, he said:

> The first images of *Amongst Women* are a park near London and a couple in it. It was near the docks. Long-distance lorry drivers used to sleep opposite the park, and in the winter the leaves would disappear off the trees and you could see as far as an artificial lake, the swings and the deer. In the summertime it was a wall of green. All that English experience, which must have been about two hundred pages, got pushed out by that Irish family, the Morans, and the London scenes with which the novel began were completely marginalized. (Ní Anluain, 2000: 149)

Clearly, the novelist is not in control of where he is going to be led. *Amongst Women* went in a completely different direction from its first images.

The Nobel Laureate, François Mauriac, maintained that his characters refused any attempts he made to convert them, that they resisted him at every turn. The independence of the material and of the characters is of the utmost importance to the integrity of the creative process. Like McGahern, Mauriac portrayed what he knew best: the gentry class of the Landes district around Bordeaux into which he was born. He managed to translate their many quirks and foibles and to allow his readers enter into their existence and share their emotions. Like McGahern also, he was very adept at capturing a local scene and depicting the impact of the landscape on his characters.

The French influence (if influence is the correct word — it's more a question of having a similar approach) can be seen also in his professed admiration for Flaubert: "The only role a writer has is to get his words right and to do that, as Flaubert said, you have to feel deeply and think clearly" (Maher, 2001: 80). McGahern often refers to writers like Beckett, Proust, Flaubert, Chekhov, Tolstoy, not forgetting Joyce and Yeats. He does this, not in order to impress, but rather as a means of illustrating that art is always a struggle, a balancing act between emotion and distance. All the writers mentioned above sought an impartial style that would "show" rather than "tell". They were rarely satisfied with their attempts in this regard: they were always looking for new and better ways of expressing their vision in an objective manner. Towards the end of an illuminating assessment of Joyce's *Dubliners*, which includes a detailed description of some of the correspondence between Flaubert and George Sand in which the former stated that the only duty of a novel is to be well-written, McGahern notes:

> Joyce does not judge. His characters live within the human constraints in space and time and within their own city. The quality of the language is more important than any system of ethics or aesthetics. Material and form are inseparable. So happy is the union of subject and object that they never become statements of any kind, but in their richness and truth are representations of particular lives — and of all life. (McGahern, 1991a: 36)

That outlines the literary project in stark terms. "Material and form are inseparable"; by achieving a harmonious "union of subject and object", the artist, remaining detached and yet controlling everything, through the representation of "par-

ticular lives", can aspire to capture something universal: "all
life". In the same article, McGahern quotes the famous phrase
of Flaubert: "the author is like God in nature, present every-
where but nowhere visible." When discussing other writers,
McGahern gives us clues as to what he sets out to capture in
his own writing. His enduring quality, and the element that
will continue to draw readers to his work long after he has
departed this earth, is precisely that marriage of material and
form, that invisible presence of the author — his "fingerprints" — which allows us sense "the pressure of a felt experience" (Maher and Kiberd, 2002: 91). The project is well
captured by Declan Kiberd:

> McGahern gives the image he receives. And the ex-
> perience comes through the words with a kind of di-
> rectness which, I think, makes for its immortality. . . . I
> think it is a sign of McGahern's integrity that he keeps
> returning to the same central, universal themes which
> emerge no matter what the shape of the story is that
> he is trying to tell. I would say that he is like those
> painters of the Renaissance who tried to do one
> painting over and over until they got it near to perfec-
> tion. (Maher and Kiberd, 2002: 91, 92)

In the pages that follow, you will be given a sketch of
McGahern's *oeuvre* to date and shown the evolution of his style
and approach. I ask you to be mindful of the fact that the material does not change too significantly: it is the style and rhythm
that give the characters and the books their universal quality.
Some will wonder what this book offers that will be different
from the excellent critical study of Denis Sampson, *Outstaring
Nature's Eye: The Fiction of John McGahern*, (Washington: Catholic University of America Press, 1993) or the more recent
book by James Whyte, *History, Myth and Ritual in the Fiction of
John McGahern: Strategies of Transcendence* (New York: Edwin
Mellen Press, 2002.) The main difference with Sampson's study

lies in the fact that it is being published some ten years later and that it attempts to show, in keeping with the main thrust of the Contemporary Irish Writers' series, how McGahern provides a voice and an image of an Irish rural society that is quickly disappearing. Whyte's book develops many interesting angles but fails to deal with the novel that confirms his approach to McGahern's fiction, namely *That They May Face the Rising Sun*. There will be many more studies of McGahern's work in the years ahead and each one will concentrate on different aspects of what is an extremely rich, if not extensive, corpus of work. This study is not meant to be exhaustive. Rather, it seeks to elucidate an integral aspect of his artistic approach as he outlines himself in his interview with Mike Murphy, echoing the sentiments of one of his favourite authors, Migual Torja: "Everything interesting begins with one person, in one place. The universal is the local without walls. The place itself has walls." (Ní Anluain, 2000: 150). I will end this introduction with a quote from McGahern's first novel, *The Barracks* (1963), where the heroine returns to the native village of her birth to find that little has changed. What would her impression be now, some four decades later, I wonder?

> The eternal medals and rosary beads were waiting on the spikes of the gate for whoever had lost them; the evergreens did not even sway in their sleep in the churchyard where bees droned between the graves from dandelion to white clover; and the laurelled path between the brown flagstones looked so worn smooth that she felt she was walking on them again with her bare feet of school confession evenings through the summer holidays. (*B*, 14)

Chapter One

Bleak Provincial Ireland: *The Barracks* and *The Dark*

The Barracks

The publication of a first novel is an important milestone in a writer's life. John McGahern burst on the scene in 1963 with the publication of *The Barracks*. He had been awarded the AE Memorial Award of the Irish Arts Council for an abstract from the novel in 1962. In 1964, following on the positive critical acclaim the book had received, he was also awarded a Macauley Fellowship, which permitted him to take a year's leave of absence from his teaching duties. One of the elements that makes this such a stunning first novel is McGahern's ability to see the world through the eyes of his protagonist, Elizabeth, a middle-aged woman married to Reegan, a widowed police sergeant with three children. Her life revolves around the many household chores for which she has responsibility as well as catering for the psychological needs of her husband, a veteran of the War of Independence. The intensity of his time as a guerrilla soldier and the senior position he held in the IRA make it difficult for Reegan to adjust to taking orders from his superior officer, Quirke, a man for whom he has no respect in any case. The simmering hostility between the two is a constant source of tension in the barracks.

The novel opens on a cold wet night in February. Reegan is out on his rounds and, when he returns, his wife knows that he will be in foul humour. The children have yet to start their homework. Elizabeth, unaware of the time, is darning a sock in the half-light. Willie, the eldest child, asks her if it is time to light the lamp — he will repeat the same question at the end of the book, this time to his father. The atmosphere is skilfully evoked in the opening pages. Even in his absence, we get a good knowledge of Reegan: we sense his impatience and unpredictability. Elizabeth urges the children to get their homework done quickly: "If your father sees a late rush at night there'll be trouble" (B, 10). Elizabeth is tired. She can feel the painful cysts in her breast and, as a former nurse, senses they may be malignant. She is at a remove from her step-children, who have never come to trust her fully. She can't compete with the memory of their dead mother. Willie's reaction, as he observes her on this evening, sums up the feelings of the children: "Not like the rich chestnut hair of his mother who had died, and the lovely face and hands that freckled in summer" (B, 10).

Elizabeth is not just a stranger to the step-children either. Her husband has no great insights into his wife's hopes and fears, the drudgery of her daily routine, her illness. To be fair, she does not hold this against him. She realises that he is too absorbed in his own problems to worry about hers:

> He'd have none of the big questions: What do you think of life or the relationships between people or any of the other things that have no real answers? He trusted all that to the priests as he trusted a sick body to the doctors and kept whatever observances that were laid down as long as they didn't clash with his own passions. (B, 64–5)

He is not portrayed as being threatening to her person and there is no evidence that he is violent towards her or the children — that side of the provincial Irish male (a recurring motif in McGahern's work) will be seen for the first time in *The Dark*. But he does need to unburden himself on his return of the latest clash between himself and Quirke. She's heard it all before and knows that it will only lead to trouble for all concerned. She remains quiet. Finally, it is time to say the Rosary and the various prayers are "repeated over and over in their relentless monotony" (B, 33). Elizabeth's mind comes back inexorably to her own hopeless situation:

> She felt tired and sick, her head thudding, and she put her hands to her breast more than once in awareness of the cysts there. She knelt with her head low between her elbows in the chair, changing positions for any distraction, the words she repeated as intrusive as dust in her mouth while the pain of weariness obtruded itself over everything that made up her consciousness. (B, 33)

This is a powerful description of the isolation of a woman alone with her pain and apprehension. There are many such insights into Elizabeth's desolation. But it never becomes the doleful tale of a dying middle-aged woman because Elizabeth is such a strong and resourceful person. She is intelligent and spiritual and is not afraid to face up to what lies ahead of her. She married Reegan[1] after the end of her affair with a doctor, Halliday, during her time as a nurse in London. Halliday suffered from depression and the relationship ended badly. He admitted: "That I used you so as not to have to face my own mess. That I seduced you because I was seduced myself by my own fucking lust" (B, 90). She found out shortly afterwards that

---

[1] She gives a rather unromantic explanation of her motivation for getting married. She found the home farm to which she returned stifling after London: "She'd not stay on this small farm among the hills, shut away from living by its pigsties and byres and the rutted lane that twisted out to the road between stone walls." (B, 16)

he had died in a car accident, which could easily have been suicide. The affair was useful in opening Elizabeth's mind about
the extent to which a person's dark side can obscure all that is
good about existence: "What the hell is all this living and dying
about anyway, Elizabeth? That's what I'd like to be told" (B,
85). Elizabeth will often have to ask herself the same question
after her cancer is diagnosed and she undergoes an operation
that proves unsuccessful. Unlike Halliday, however, she finds
some answers to the existential question that he posed. Not,
however, before she has to endure false hope, severe physical
and mental torture, joy at the beauty of nature and sadness at
the knowledge that she will soon have to leave it all behind:

> Whether she had cancer or not wasn't her whole life a
> waiting, the end would arrive sooner or later, twenty
> extra years meant nothing to the dead, but, no, no, no.
> She couldn't face it. Time was only for the living. She
> wanted time, as much time as she could get. (B, 72)

Through a series of interior monologues and flashbacks,
we come to know Elizabeth intimately and to see existence
through her eyes. McGahern has acknowledged, in fact, that
"Elizabeth was as much a way of looking as a character in her
own right" (Kennedy, 1984: 40). Reading the novel is cathar-
tic in the sense that we experience the tragedy of the end of
Elizabeth's life but are not obliged to undergo firsthand the
awful reality her death represents for her. After her husband
brings her to the hospital for what will turn out to be a stay
of a few months, she is left alone to cope with the anguish of
her bruised and deformed body — the medical team were
forced to perform a mastectomy.

She realises that the most effective way to beat the pain is
by employing her mind, and especially her memory: "She was
not really going in a common taxi to a common death. She
had a rich life, and she could remember" (B, 115). Memory
will be an important device in helping McGahern's characters

to cope with life. Most of the time, the "remembered" past assumes a romantic glow that is created by distance. Elizabeth's life does not seem in any way "rich" to readers at the opening of the novel: it appears humdrum and monotonous.

But what is beyond dispute is her strong faith, a faith she nurtured at a slight remove from the official church. She had enough independence of spirit to resist the efforts of the parish priest who wanted her to join the local branch of the Legion of Mary: "a kind of legalized gossiping school to the women and a convenient pool of labour that the priests could draw on for catering committees" (B, 163). What appealed to her about her religion was "the church services, always beautiful, especially in Holy Week; witnessed so often in the same unchanging pattern that they didn't come in broken recollections but flowed before the mind with the calm and grace and reassurance of all ritual" (B, 123).[2] The clergy she sees as being the flawed human beings that we all are. Thus, she likes to travel to the church on different occasions when she is in town on some errand. She doesn't seek a solution to her problems from religion: "There were no answers . . . she'd no business to be in the church except she loved it and it was quiet" (B, 165).

Elizabeth is a strong woman who ends up accepting her mortality with dignity. When she is faced with the reality of dying, the appeal of the imperfect world strikes her with some force. One morning she looks out the window and sees with the eyes of the dying person the beauty that is all around her:

> It was so beautiful when she let the blinds up first thing that, "Jesus Christ", softly was all she was able

---

[2] Jean-Michel Ganteau makes the point that Elizabeth is first presented as an unbeliever, as someone who has been deeply marked by Halliday's atheism and his belief in the absence of meaning in existence: "Despite a certain number of relapses, she is subsequently drawn towards the acceptance of faith. She grows resigned to the impalpable substance of religious belief and ponders on the close relationship between faith and doubt" (Ganteau, 1995: 37).

> to articulate as she looked out and up the river to the
> woods across the lake, black with the leaves fallen ex-
> cept the red rust of beech trees, the withered leaves
> standing pale and sharp as bamboo rods at the edges
> of the water. (B, 170)

This familiar scene, to which, when healthy, she had scarcely paid any attention, is now firmly etched on her conscious-ness. When questioned about this episode, McGahern stated: "When you're in danger of losing a thing it becomes precious and when it's all around us, it's in tedious abundance and we take it for granted as if we're going to live forever, which we're not" (Maher, 2001: 75). The familiar countryside is a soothing presence in the book, as well as being a source of nostalgia. When looking out from the window of a train (a regular vantage point for characters in McGahern's fiction) as she travels to hospital, the banal sights assume a heightened significance for Elizabeth: "Trees, fields, houses, telegraph-poles jerking on wires, thorn hedges, cattle, sheep, men, women, horses and sows with their litters started to move across the calm glass" (B, 112). There is a type of incantatory quality to the writing here, a desire to name and to celebrate the ordinary. It is as though McGahern wants to record in a systematic manner what Elizabeth, with her heightened vision, sees. She plays the role of the writer here, in a sense. She is wording the world, naming things, places and people.

She is aware of the seasons changing. The religious cere-monies mark the different times of year. (We will see this concentration on how religious rituals mirror the passing of the seasons to a marked degree also in *That They May Face the Rising Sun.*) On Christmas night, Elizabeth and Reegan make love — a scene that caused turmoil among some readers who felt that the religious feast and such a description should not have been mentioned in the same breath: "They'd try to fall apart without noticing much wrench, and lie in the animal warmth and loving kindness of each other against the silence of the room" (*B*, 181). Their last Christmas dinner together assumes a sacramental quality: "Never did the table-cloth appear so bright as this day. . . . and the meal began and ended in the highest form of all celebration, prayer" (*B*, 183). After Christmas comes the beginning of Lent, with its symbolism of fast and abstinence and its emphasis on the fragility of the human body: "Ash Wednesday, a cold white morning, all the villagers at mass and the rails, to be signed with the Cross on their lives to be broken, all sinners and needing the grace of God to be saved, the cross thumbed by the priests on their foreheads with the ashes of their mortality" (*B*, 194). Elizabeth knows that she is beginning her last few weeks before she has to climb Golgotha. The Stations of the Cross thus assume a real poignancy for her:

> She saw her own life declared in them and made known, the unendurable pettiness and degradation of her own feelings raised to dignity and meaning in Christ's passion. (B, 194)

At Easter, she ruminates on how the Resurrection and the Ascension "seemed shadowy and unreal compared to the way of Calvary" (*B*, 195). She is confined to bed in the barracks where the sounds of the outside world touch her in a hitherto unknown part of her being:

> Outside the morning was clean and cold, men after hot breakfasts were on their way to work. The noises of the morning rose within her to a call of wild excitement. Never had she felt it so when she was rising to let up the blinds in the kitchen . . . and now it was a wild call to life, life, life and life at any cost. (B, 201–2)

Where are the images of bleak provincial Ireland, you may ask? Well, they can be seen in almost every stage of Elizabeth's illness. Her struggle with cancer is mirrored by her husband's frantic attempts to save as much turf as possible to enable him to pay the medical bills and to buy himself a small farm. He thinks he will then be happy because freed from a job he despises. He cannot endure his present life much longer. The thought of losing a second wife is too much for him to contemplate.[3] So he spends as much time as possible away from her. She marvels at how poorly she knows him: "He was a strange person, she hardly knew anything about him, beyond the mere physical acts of intimacy" (B, 64). She understands that she can expect limited support from this source. It is her spirituality, her unflinching faith that provides her with some limited solace. Elizabeth is the most religious of all McGahern's characters. She has a huge attachment to rituals and ceremonies.[4] At times she is unaware of the prayers she is saying or the meaning of the ceremonies. Everything happens at a deeper level: mysteries are not supposed to be understood:

> The rosary had grown into her life: she'd come to love its words, its rhythm, its repetitions, its confident chanting, its eternal mysteries; what it meant didn't matter . . . it gave the last need of her heart release, the need to praise and celebrate, in which everything rejoiced. (B, 220)

When Elizabeth passes away, there is a great moment when the two guards, Mullins and Casey, slip away to the nearby

---

[3] Rüdiger Imhof brings out the contrast between Reegan's suffering and that of his wife in the following terms: "*The Barracks* is at once a deeply distressing and indeed liberating book that gains in impact by juxtaposing Elizabeth's fight for her life and Reegan's fight against Quirke, the one a quintessentially existentialist fight and the other a petty fight. Reegan sees his own case in such an existential dimension that he has no time to discern the full horror of his wife's plight." (Imhof, 2002: 217)

[4] McGahern passed from this deep spiritual exegesis to the pagan humanity that characterises *That They May Face the Rising Sun* where religious practices are only mentioned in passing.

Protestant cemetery, Eastersnow. Being situated in the West of
Ireland, the Protestant graveyard is thinly populated. The two
men, both attached to Elizabeth when she was alive, feel relief
at the fact that it is she, and not they, who has died. Behind
them they can hear the sound of the clay thudding against the
coffin and they cannot hide their feeling of satisfaction:

> "It's Elizabeth that's being covered and not me and
> I'm able to stand in the sun and watch", not able to
> take the upper hand in their minds till they got the
> bulk of the stone church between themselves and the
> grave. (B, 223)

Their reaction is a human one and typical of how many people feel when they are attending funerals. The number of cars
that are seen following the funeral cortege is taken as a sign
of the importance of the person being buried. Elizabeth had a
satisfactory number following hers.

Throughout her illness, Elizabeth is aware of all that is happening in the world beyond her bedroom. The sounds of nature and of human activity tell her all she needs to know about
the outside world — of particular significance in this regard are
the sounds coming from the local sawmill and the comings and
goings in the barracks and on the streets.

After her burial, there is one remaining issue that needs
closure in the novel and that is the enmity between Reegan and
Quirke. The former does nothing to avoid the confrontation
that is looming. He does not turn up for duty on time and on
the rare occasions he is seen, he is neither shaved nor properly
dressed. Sensing that he has pushed things to the limit, he hands
in his resignation before telling the Superintendent what he
really thinks of him. All the years of frustration find expression
in the verbal assault he unleashes when told that he will be dis-
ciplined. He refers to his experience as a freedom fighter and
contrasts it to the command that Quirke now exercises:

> I wore the Sam Browne too, the one time it was dangerous to wear it in this balls of a country. And I wore it to command men, soldiers, and not to motor round to see if a few harmless poor bastards would lick me fat arse, while I shit about law and order. (B, 231)

Elizabeth's death does not resolve any problems. Reegan doesn't have the money he needs to buy a farm. Once more, his children have no mother to look after them. The wheel comes full circle as Willie asks his father if it is time to light the lamp on the last page of the book. Thomas Kilroy provides an excellent analysis of the atmosphere of The Barracks, which he calls the "withering constriction, the landscape of inhibition" (Kilroy, 1972: 302). The message is really quite simple: life is unchanging for most people; there are many detours on the way but we inevitably end up back where we started, with the realisation that we haven't discovered much about the mystery of life: "It all came round if you could manage to survive long enough" (B, 66). Elizabeth does get some insights into the meaning or the meaninglessness of her existence. She achieves peace when she stops fighting against what she cannot control. In her provincial isolation, memory, religion and nature provide her with the means to endure her desolate fate.

McGahern's first novel showed many of the talents he was to hone as his career progressed. In spite of the pervading atmosphere of stasis and paralysis in provincial life, there is also the powerful celebration of living with intensity. Jürgen Kamm sums it up well:

> The Barracks is in many ways a masterly achievement. The blending of its universal thematic concerns with a specifically Irish setting which is rendered with great precision and attention to detail is entirely convincing. Likewise, the central character's quest for meaning, purpose and identity is aesthetically realized by the adroit handling of flashbacks, interior monologue and

stream-of-consciousness technique, thus imparting to the reader both Elizabeth's isolation and her frantic groping for truth. (Kamm, 1990: 180)

The Dark

The tone of the second novel, *The Dark*, as its title suggests, is unappetising in that it portrays a most repressive image of Irish provincial life. It reveals a cruel, often secret facet of rural life in Ireland where the father could be sadistic to, and abusive of, his children. Aesthetically, it is also somewhat more problematic than *The Barracks*, as we shall see. The opening scene is one of the most horrific I have ever read. The main character, Mahoney (we are never given his first name), has been heard to utter an oath under his breath and his father, in a mad rage, instructs him to remove his clothes and bend over a chair. He then proceeds to simulate a beating by striking the ground beside his son:

> He couldn't control his water and it flowed from him over the leather of the seat. He'd never imagined horror such as this, waiting naked for the leather to come down on his flesh, would it ever come, it was impossible and yet nothing could be worse than this waiting. (D, 9)

Mahoney senior is a brutish widower who is clearly aroused by inflicting this sort of ritual on his son. He observes the boy's discomfiture with satisfaction: "He didn't lift a hand, as if the stripping compelled by his will alone gave him pleasure" (D, 8).

The Dark evokes an unappetising and, at the time of its publication, a hidden face of provincial Ireland. There are few, if any, of the descriptions of the beauty of nature and the joys of ritual that we encounter in *The Barracks*. Everything is couched in an atmosphere of fear and loathing. The children are united in their hatred of their father: "They all got beatings, often for no reason, because they laughed when he was in foul humour but they learned to make him suffer — to close their life against him and to leave him to himself" (D, 11).

Worse than the beatings is the sexual abuse. The main character is forced to share a bed with his father and, when he tries to feign sleep, his father lights matches up against his eyes. Then come the "dirty rags of intimacy" (D, 19). The father strokes his son's stomach and genitalia, causing both to reach orgasm. The following passage captures in graphic terms the type of perversity that was unmentionable in this country until recently:

> The words drummed softly as the stroking hands moved on his belly, down and up, touched with the fingers the thighs again, and came again on the back.
> "You like that. It's good for you, the voice breathed jerkily now to the stroking hands.
> "I like that."
> There was nothing else to say, it was better not to think or care. (D, 20)

This is the type of description that probably led to the banning of the book — it was most daring for the time. It is easy to forget that the novel was published in the middle of the 1960s, at a time when the Irish Republic was ruled like a theocracy and the Catholic Church, though challenged more than it had been in the early decades of the century, still wielded a huge amount of power and influence. The boy's bouts of masturbation seem very mild by comparison with the paternal abuse. And yet it is the masturbation that causes him to doubt his worthiness for the priesthood. There is a pervading sense of sinfulness and decay throughout the narrative.

The hero, or anti-hero, is undergoing the difficult process of growing to independence in the shadow of a father who is loath to see him escape from his power. He places obstacles in the way of his studies, making noise downstairs when he knows that the boy is working in the room above. The idea of a son gaining a university scholarship rankles with a man who never got past primary school — he is at pains to point out, however, that he and another boy had been the best students in their class. There is pride in the achievement of his son when the scholarship does come his way, but then it is complete overkill. They go to buy the young man a new suit, tell the whole village about his success and go for a celebratory meal in the Royal Hotel. But, as we are told: "there was no union between them" (*D*, 157). Nevertheless, as they travel home that evening and pass in front of the graveyard, the father's comment elicits a positive reaction from young Mahoney:

> "It gives me the creeps that place! No matter what happens it winds up there. And you wouldn't mind but there's people dying to get into it," everybody repeated themselves but suddenly at the old joke he wanted to laugh with him and say,
> "You are marvellous, my father." (*D*, 160)

Every child wants to love his father but there are times in *The Dark* when one wonders how the young man could be forgiving of someone who had inflicted so much psychological damage on him.

The masturbation is a momentary release from the harrowing reality that is all around him: "Everything is dead as dirt, it is as easy to turn over. I'd committed five sins since morning" (*D*, 31). He looks on his body as something dirty, the playground of the devil. He cannot see how someone as impure as he could aspire to becoming a priest. He had made a promise to his dying mother that one day he would say Mass for her and the sight of her Memoriam card triggers off the memory of this promise:

> On the road as I came with her from town loaded with parcels and the smell of tar in the heat I'd prom-

> ised that one day I'd say Mass for her. And all I did for
> her now was listen to my father's nagging and carry
> on private orgies of abuse. (*D*, 23)

One of the main attractions of the priestly calling is that, by foregoing all pleasures other than spiritual ones, he was booking a place in Heaven. After Confession, there is the elation of having wiped the slate clean: "Such relief had come to you, fear and darkness gone, never would you sin again. The pleasures seemed so mean and grimy against the sheer delight of peace, pure as snow in the air" (*D*, 42). McGahern has emphasised that, for him, the injurious aspect of Irish Catholicism is to be found in its attitude to sexuality. Certainly, there was a tendency to concentrate almost exclusively on the sins of the flesh and on the fires of Hell (again Joyce highlighted this in *A Portrait of the Artist as a Young Man*). Thus, the young man contemplates eternity with some foreboding:

> The moment of death was the one real moment in
> life; everything took its proper position there, and
> was fixed for ever, whether to live in joy or hell for all
> eternity, or had your life been the haphazard flicker
> between nothingness and nothingness. (*D*, 69)

This passage conveys in a forceful way the fear of a young man as he contemplates the loss of his soul for eternity. Were he able to control his sexual urges and to devote his life to God, he could more easily ensure that his life would not be "the haphazard flicker between nothingness and nothingness".

The summer before he sits his Leaving Cert., he is invited to spend some time with a cousin, Fr Gerald, who has also arranged a position for Mahoney's sister with a family in his parish, the Ryans. They stop off at this house before going to the presbytery. Mahoney is disturbed by his sister's appearance and especially by her comment: "It's worse than home" (*D*, 63). Later he discovers that Mr Ryan has been bothering her. Fr Gerald enters the boy's room late that night on the pretext of discussing his vocation with him. He gets in bed alongside him. The narration has changed to the second person singular as the boy attempts to analyse his feelings:

> . . . you stiffened when his arm went around your shoulder, was this to be another of the midnight horrors with your father. His hand closed on your arm. You wanted to curse or wrench yourself free but you had to lie stiff as a board, stare straight ahead at the wall, afraid before anything of meeting the eyes you knew were searching your face. (*D*, 70–1)

Nothing untoward happens on this occasion.[5] Fr Gerald asks Mahoney if he has made any decision about the priesthood. On sensing the hesitation, he begins to explore in an intrusive manner the reasons for his indecision. He asks leading questions as though they were in the confessional: Has he ever desired to kiss a girl? Did he excite himself at the thought? Cause seed to spill in his excitement? The priest knows the terrain he is exploring and is abusing his authority. When asked if he ever had to fight the sin of masturbation himself when he was Mahoney's age, Fr Gerald says nothing: "There was such silence that you winced" (*D*, 73). The boy feels doubly betrayed by the fact that his confession has not secured at least some semblance of a response from the priest. Then comes anger:

> What right had he to come and lie with you in bed, his body hot against yours, his arm around your shoulders. Almost as the cursed nights when your father used stroke your thighs. (*D*, 74)

---

[5] One is left wondering what is the nature of the relationship between Fr. Gerald and the young fifteen-year-old boy who keeps house for him. Certainly, it is not a situation that could be countenanced today.

The young man is beginning to see a pattern to the abuse that he has been made to endure and is kicking against it. After this incident, he abandons all thoughts of the priesthood. It is true that when he tells Fr Gerald of his decision the latter makes a most compelling argument about the good that can be achieved by a successful ministry in the Church. But it is too late then. The attraction of the priesthood was great for young Mahoney. He would have had respect, standing, a feeling of being a force for good. All this seemed far more attractive than simply living out a few sordid dreams with a woman:

> Death would come. Everything riveted into that. Possession of neither a world nor a woman mattered then, whether you could go to the Judgment or not without flinching was all that would matter. I strove as fierce as I was able, would be a lot to be able to say. A priest could say that. He'd chosen God before life. (D, 83)

Having turned his back on the priesthood, it takes on all the appeal of what he can never have. Mahoney is a stunted character who never achieves the understanding of existence that Elizabeth reaches. That, of course, has much to do with his age — he is far younger than she — and the unfortunate upbringing he had. He is certainly the victim of a repressive religion that emphasises the sins of the flesh to an unhealthy degree. Then his father's abuse and the betrayal of his cousin do not help him in any way to find liberation from his feelings of sinfulness. One of his few fine moments in the novel is the liberation of his sister, Joan, from the clutches of the Ryans. He insists that she come home with him, in spite of the displeasure of Mrs Ryan in particular who may well suspect the reason for Joan's departure was her desire to escape from the lascivious attentions of Mr Ryan. Social respectability ensures that Fr Gerald will not question the Ryans about what went on with his cousin — they are among the biggest contributors to the Church in the parish.

The end of *The Dark* has been the source of some dissatisfaction to critics like John Cronin — we'll discuss the latter's view in a moment. Firstly, I will give a short résumé of what happens. Mahoney wins the university scholarship but also has an offer of a job in the ESB. He opts for the former and heads to Galway. The previous summer has seen him grow to manhood — he can now put in a better day's work than his father who has grown old: "What was strange to notice was that Mahoney was growing old. He'd stop and lean on the pick, panting" (D, 149). He doesn't pose any physical threat any more. The son, in contrast, is blossoming: "There was the delight of power and ease in every muscle now, he'd grown fit and hard, he'd worked in the unawareness of a man's day" (D, 148). The joy he finds working in the fields is not matched anywhere else in his life. In fact, it may well be that becoming a farmer, like his father, might have offered him the best chance of happiness. One might reasonably expect that his physical maturity be matched by an emotional and intellectual flowering. University should have provided the liberation from his father's repressive influence that the boy craved as an adolescent. There were girls in abundance and the studies should not have been a problem to a scholarship boy like himself. Two episodes render the experience in Galway a disappointment. The first is his expulsion from a lecture theatre by a lecturer who always picked on someone in such an arbitrary fashion at the beginning of the academic year. The second is his failure to even enter the Aula where the Jibs' Dance is taking place. He had been painstaking in his preparations, had applied the Brylcream, washed his teeth, put on his new suit. He sees the irony of his situation:

> This was the dream you'd left the stern and certain
> road of the priesthood to follow after, that road so
> attractive now since you hadn't to face walking it any
> more, and this world of sensuality from which you

> were ready to lose your soul not so easy to drag to
> your mouth either for that one destructive kiss, as
> hard to lose your soul as to save it. (D, 177–8)

This passage is written in an unusually awkward style. The
reader knows what the hero is trying to express, his hesitations
and doubts, his insecurity about asking girls up to dance, maybe
getting to kiss them, opening himself out to the world of sexuality, but normally McGahern conveys these feelings in a more
precise manner. Then there's the volte-face and the decision to
take up the job in the ESB after all. His father is summoned to
Galway, spends the night with his son in the digs, speaks to his
tutor and supports him in his decision to leave. Then there's a
moment of epiphany that is not really an epiphany:

> You were walking through the rain of Galway with your
> father and you could laugh purely, without bitterness,
> for the first time and it was a kind of happiness, at its
> heart the terror of an unclear recognition of the reality
> that set you free, touching you with as much foreboding
> as the sodden leaves falling in this day, or any cliché.

The style is again imprecise here — the sentence never gets to
its natural destination. I do not follow the sudden change in the
attitude of the young man to his father. John Cronin presents
this view: "There is an inconsistency of character and incident
here . . . the novelist fails utterly to justify this particular epiphany" (Cronin, 1969: 429). The critic questioned the author on
this subject after he did a reading from The Dark at the 1967
Belfast Festival: "I suggested that he might have failed to resolve the logic of the boy's situation in this passage. It seemed
to me that he had left his character on the question without
knowing the answer, that the author had lost objectivity and
control" (Cronin, 1969: 429). Here I am not fully in agreement
with the critic. I imagine that McGahern's response would be
that it is not the novelist's function to pronounce on these issues, that it is up to the reader to assess whether it works or

not. Cronin is correct to point out a number of inconsistencies in the narrative pattern and in the evolution of Mahoney's character but perhaps what happens at the end of the novel was out of McGahern's control. The jerky style and fluctuating points of view could be a means of translating the uncertainty and insecurity of a young man who is unable to embrace change. McGahern did point out in his reply to Cronin that "he found it impossible to take a hopeful view of the universe — there is no pie in his sky, only dark clouds through which, occasionally, an unexplained sun unexpectedly gleams" (Cronin, 1969: 430). My reservations have mainly to do with some awkward sentences and the general confusion that surrounds the hero's decision to abandon university and to suddenly reconcile himself with his father. I don't know if he could readily forgive the man who abused him so horribly: "I wouldn't have been brought up any other way or by any other father" (*D*, 191). Having reached this reconciliation, the two go to bed:

> It seemed that the whole world must turn over in the
> night and howl in its boredom, for the father and the
> son and for the whole shoot, but it did not. (*D*, 191)

There is no resolution to the problems that young Mahoney faces provided here. It is important to note that the point of view used throughout most of this novel is that of a confused child. Sometimes McGahern manages to convey this confusion very well, without ever achieving the mastery of a McCourt in this area. When it comes to dealing with the sexual abuse, young Mahoney seems to bury what's happening him in his unconscious. We're not sure what the quote above is supposed to mean. Certainly, the young man's problems are far from being resolved by his decision to take up the position in Dublin. The whole world does not "howl in its boredom", but what awaits him in the capital is precisely that same "boredom" from which he wanted to escape earlier but which he now freely chooses.

The first period in McGahern's evolution is marked by an impressive first novel in which subject matter and form attain a good balance. The second novel, which announces some of the experimentation with form that will dominate the next two novels, is less convincing on many levels. That said, it contains some keen insights into the provincial Ireland of the 1950s and '60s. There is also some bitterness, however, which could account for the less than convincing conclusion to the novel. McGahern may have been helped by seeing the world through a woman's eyes in *The Barracks* — this allowed him to maintain a certain distance. The fact that *The Dark* is a *bildungsroman* (the portrait of an artist as a young man) may have unconsciously led McGahern into territory that didn't quite suit his artistic temperament. Kamm notes that the novel is fraught with autobiographical experiences — McGahern admitted in an interview with Eileen Kennedy that during his years as a student with the Presentation Brothers in Carrick-on-Shannon he thought about becoming a priest — and he adds:

> *The Dark* lacks distance because the writer comes precariously close to his own youth, and although young Mahoney's Christian name is never disclosed, there is reason to believe it could be John. (Kamm, 1990: 182–3)

But any slight reservation one may entertain with regard to the harmony or disharmony of the narrative cannot take away from the courage with which McGahern exposes a hidden Ireland that is characterised by psychological and sexual abuse, an unhealthy preoccupation with the sins of the flesh, a guilt-ridden and pious population and a manipulative Catholic clergy. We may have preferred not to know that this Ireland existed but recent revelations about industrial schools, orphanages, clerical sex abuse, sex abuse within the home, can leave us in no doubt that it did. Now that McGahern had found his voice with his first fictions, we will see how he continued to refine and polish it in the next stage of his literary evolution.

Chapter Two

Experiments with Style: *The Leavetaking* and *The Pornographer*

The Leavetaking

We saw some of the more problematic aspects that McGahern encountered in giving an authentic voice to his hero in *The Dark*. In that regard, it is fair to say that he had already embarked on an experimental path with regard to style in his second novel. *The Leavetaking* was first published in 1974 and McGahern, following his re-reading of the novel in the light of Alain Delahaye's French translation, undertook a second and significantly improved version that was published in 1984.[1] I am going to confine my discussion to the later version and show how, for the first time in McGahern's fiction, there is a brightening of the landscape and a possibility of the main character achieving fulfilment through a healthy sexual rela-

---

[1] He gives the background to this decision in the interview at the end of this book. Two excellent articles by Marianne Mays and Terence Killeen deal with the style of *The Leavetaking* in some detail in the July 1991 edition of *The Canadian Journal of Irish Studies*. The former takes extracts from the 1974 edition and shows how they were edited and shortened to telling effect in the later version. ("'Ravished and Exasperated': The Evolution of John McGahern's Plain Style", pp. 38–52).

tionship with a woman. The subject matter of the book, dealing as it does with the sacking of a primary school teacher
because of the discovery that he married a Protestant in a
registry office, has clear autobiographical overtones that can
at times be injurious to the objectivity of the narrator.

In the Preface to the second edition, McGahern makes some
pertinent points. He first of all says that the novel was written as
a love story, its two parts deliberately different in style:

> It was an attempt to reflect the purity of feeling with
> which all the remembered "I" comes to us, the banal
> and the precious alike; and yet how that more than "I"
> — the beloved, the "otherest", the most trusted mo-
> ments of that life — stumbles continually away from us
> as poor reportage, and to see if these disparates could
> in any way be made true to one another. (*L*, 5)

He is preoccupied with the Proustian idea of "memory regained", or Wordsworth's theory in *Tintern Abbey* of how the
poet must aspire to "see into the life of things". "Emotion recollected in tranquillity" is a basic tenet of Wordsworth's concept of the artistic vision and it is one which McGahern clearly
saw as being important to his novelistic approach. He admits
that his main problem with *The Leavetaking* was that he was
too close to the "more than 'I'", the "most trusted moments":

> The crudity I was attempting to portray, the irre-
> deemable imprisonment of the beloved in reportage,
> had itself become blatant. I had been too close to the
> "Idea", and the work lacked that distance, that inner
> formality or calm, that all writing, no matter what it is
> attempting, must possess. (*L*, 5)

Such a statement is vital to our understanding of McGahern's
evolution as a novelist. I believe that he could have applied
this critique equally well to *The Dark* as to *The Leavetaking*. It
is significant that he should see the dangers involved in getting

too close to the "Idea" and that he would view "that inner formality or calm" as being a prerequisite for all good writing. He achieves that objectivity in his later novels, especially in *Amongst Women*, as we shall see. He doesn't quite manage it in the two novels that we are going to discuss in this chapter, even though they do represent a move in the right direction.

The Leavetaking is divided into two parts, the first of which describes the death of the narrator's mother and his double guilt of not having spent the vital last hour at her bedside before he is sent away to be with his father in the barracks[2] and of not fulfilling her dying wish that one day he would say Mass for her. (This is very close to young Mahoney's promise to his mother in *The Dark*.) There is a close relationship between the mother and her first-born. The father feels neglected after the birth. The attentions of his wife and mother seem totally focused on the baby. He is a manipulator, a self-centred egotist like many of McGahern's father figures:

> "The child is ruined past correction. You've ruined him and let the old woman ruin him", he scolded before leaving for the barracks while the grandmother comforted the child in the bedroom. (*L*, 47)

All these memories flash through Patrick Moran's mind during his last day in school before his imminent dismissal.[3] We get

---

[2] Children of a dying parent are usually sent away so as not to witness the death and are not allowed attend the funeral in McGahern's novels. The Reegan children's experience with their biological mother in *The Barracks* is typical of this custom: "They hadn't seen coffin or hearse or anything. She'd been taken from the hospital to the church in the evening and buried the next afternoon." (*B*, 102)

[3] Terence Killeen maintains that "narrative suspense" is impaired by letting readers know from the beginning that Patrick Moran is to be dismissed from his post: "When the novelist dispenses with this elementary device for holding the reader's attention, a very powerful alternative has to be put

varying perspectives or points of view, as can be seen in the
lines just quoted about the father's reaction. At times, we
have access to the feelings of the mother also, though it has
to be said that we are never privy to what emotions either
parent is really experiencing. The "I" narrator, as is normal, is
mainly concerned with conveying his own memories. Primary
among them is the death of his mother. The novel opens with
the teacher supervising the schoolyard:

> I watch a gull's shadow float among the feet on the
> concrete as I walk in a day of my life with a bell, its
> brass tongue in my hand, and think after all that the
> first constant was water. (*L*, 9)

The concluding image of the book is of water also — another
circular movement in McGahern's fiction. Note how the reverie of the narrator is evoked through the shadow of the gull
mingling with the children's feet.[4] He is physically present,
carrying out a duty with which he is totally familiar (the brass
tongue has often been felt in the palm of his hand before).
Because his gestures and movements are automatic, the narrator can allow his mind to wander and still perform his duties adequately. All the time, he is conscious of the woman in
his life who is waiting for him in their digs in Howth and who
is in some ways the mirror image of his mother. On returning

---

in its place." He adds: "In a work such as this, imagery has to carry much of
the burden that would normally fall on characterization and narrative." The
imagery is strong in the novel and does compensate to a large extent for
the lack of narrative suspense. (Cf. "Versions of Exile: A Reading of *The
Leavetaking*" in *Canadian Journal of Irish Studies*, July 1991, 70–1.)

[4] Anne Goarzin maintains that the cries of the gulls provide a kind of backdrop to the sound of the children's feet on the concrete and subsequently
to that of the Headmaster's voice and the bell ringing that controls the
various rituals in the yard. Goarzin also does an excellent analysis of how
the opening and concluding paragraphs of the novel complement each
other (Goarzin, 2002: 122-4).

from England, the couple went for a walk on the hill of Howth, thus repeating the itinerary of his mother and father on their honeymoon. Her first experience of sexual intercourse was not pleasant:

> "Has it happened to me?" was all her mind could frame over the tea and toast and brown bread of the North Star Hotel breakfast the next morning, the mind already trying to change the sheets and blood and sexual suck of the night into a sacrificial marble on which a cross stood in the centre of tulips and white candles. (*L*, 42)

This was a highly spiritual woman who had been seriously tempted by a religious vocation. Her husband had pursued her relentlessly until she agreed to marriage. Note how the contrast is drawn between the blood of her lost virginity and the cross. The white candles seem to offer a nostalgic image of a purity that has been lost in the physical coupling. There is no linear development in the plot of *The Leavetaking*, which reflects the jumbled manner in which the memories come to the young teacher. The strongest image of all concerns the removal of the furniture and the children from his mother's house to the barracks. Like Reegan before him, the father in this instance does not spend her last days with his wife, much to the disgust of his brother-in-law, Michael. The driver of the lorry who is sent to collect the furniture hands Michael a note: "It just says he's sorry he couldn't come because of duty" (*L*, 70). There is annoyance among her family that he should insist on this operation being carried out with such urgency: "If that bloody man was only halfnatural and left the house as it was for a time", our uncle muttered (*L*, 71). After all, the father had been directly responsible for his wife's condition. They had been told that it would be dangerous for her to conceive another child. That didn't stop him the fatal night he cycled the long distance in the rain to her cottage from the barracks:

"Is it all right?" he drew her to him.

"It's a dangerous time."

"I'll be careful", starved for sexuality he could not hold back.

She turned to him: it was her duty. (*L*, 65)

There is a harsh realism in the lines above. The reaction of Patrick's mother, her submissiveness to her husband's needs, the careless way the father puts her life in jeopardy just to satisfy his lust, all are well captured. Because of this event, Patrick must bear the loss of his refuge, the first love of his life. The goodbye between them is the most poignant moment of the book:

> "I came to say goodbye, mother," the priest had a hand on my shoulder as I bent to kiss her, and as lips touched everything was burned away except that I had to leave at once. If I stayed one moment longer I was lost. Panic was growing: to put arms about the leg of the bed so that they'd not be able to drag me away, to stay by that bed forever. (*L*, 71)

There is good control displayed in the writing here in spite of the deep emotion that is being conveyed. There must be at least some connection between this description and the death of McGahern's own mother. The "inner formality and calm" that he mentioned in his Preface is in evidence as well as his undoubted skill at depicting the scene as it was lived through the eyes of the child. The strongest image of the whole book is the one that follows shortly after the last goodbye has taken place and it reverberates throughout the narrative. The turmoil in the young boy's heart is echoed by the sounds of hammering that fill the house:

> The beating apart of the beds rang through the house, rusted at the joinings by damp; the thin walls shivered

> at each beat, and the picture of the Sacred Heart
> swayed on its cord. (*L*, 71)

This is a key moment in the boy's consciousness — he will
repeatedly hear the sound of the wrenching apart of the beds
in later life. He feels outrage that his mother should be exposed to this insensitivity and at the same time he knows that
he has failed her also in her hour of greatest need. Instead of
staying in the bedroom, he had gone out into the yard: "O
but if only I could have had back then that whole hour I had
wasted down with the lorry on the cinders so that I could
see her stir or smile. I would portion the hour out so that I
would see her forever" (*L*, 75). To add to his discomfiture, he
realises that the promise he made to her to become a priest
never materialised and will not do so now. He had felt at the
time of her death that he would fulfil the promise: "One day I
would say Mass for her soul" (*L*, 44). The lure of the flesh was
too strong and would not be denied.

The voice of Patrick Moran is authentic and consistent,
and there is no attempt to sanitise the raw pain that he feels
as he remembers his last moments with his mother. When he
is staying at the barracks where his father is stationed after
her death, he watches the clock all day and imagines what is
happening at the funeral:

> Once the hands passed five I grew feverish as I pic-
> tured the house. The brown coffin would come in the
> glass of the hearse. People would leave the house and
> gather outside as soon as they looked in the empty
> coffin. The doors would be shut, the blinds of the
> window drawn. (*L*, 78)

Again, this is a most realistic portrayal of how a child would
recreate in his mind the various stages in the burial of his
mother.

The first part of the book does an excellent job of capturing the memories of childhood as they flood into the mind of
Patrick. The pace is maintained throughout; the images are
strong and convincing. With Part II, however, this quality is
not maintained as the narrator moves into a description of his
relationship with Isobel and attempts to analyse how his past
has impacted on it. The last paragraph of Part I sets the scene:

> The shadow had fallen on the life and would shape it
> as the salt and wind shaped the trees the sea lord had
> planted as shelter against the sea: and part of that
> shaping lead to the schoolroom of this day, but by
> evening the life would have made its last break with
> the shadow, and would be free to grow without warp
> in its own light. (L, 82)

There is some optimism in these lines. It seems as though he
has made a significant stand in favour of freedom. However,
the second part opens with the line: "One day I'd say Mass
for her" (L, 85), which shows that the obsession with the
priesthood has not yet left him. The reason he could not fulfil
his promise to his mother was that he met Isobel and fell in
love with her. He wanted to make it up to his mother for the
betrayal at her bedside when she was dying: "but that in its
turn became the sacrifice of the dream of another woman,
became the death in life, the beginning only in the end" (L,
85). Isobel was one of a stream of women with whom he had
fallen in love or made love. When Dublin and teaching became tedious for him, he got a year's leave of absence and
found work as a barman in London. Meeting Isobel was the
beginning of a new phase. She too had been wounded by life
— her father sexually abused her as a child and, although she
is now an adult, he still tries to control her. Patrick and Isobel
attempt to assist each other in escaping from a painful past.

It has been noted, with some justification, that the secondary characters in *The Leavetaking* lack depth[5] and certainly the writing, when the narrator travels to London, is less than sure. Mention of London pubs and the various landmarks of the English capital do not have the same ring as Drumshambo and Aughoo and the other Irish placenames that intersperse the narrative. I would argue that that is because McGahern's sense of place is rooted in rural Ireland and that his most successful dramas are acted out in that setting. Eileen Kennedy makes the point: "The scenes in London are lively but unconvincing: McGahern's strength lies in his treatment of Irish figures and especially the rural landscape" (Kennedy, 1983: 122).

It is sometimes difficult to ascertain what is so special about Patrick's relationship with Isobel. Why is she so different from the other women with whom he has had relationships? What leads him to get married in full knowledge of the negative consequences it will have on his career? I don't think any of these questions are adequately answered.

When he discusses the events surrounding his dismissal, in places it becomes almost indistinguishable from autobiography. The Manager of the school, Fr Curry, from whom he receives his formal dismissal, gives out about doctors in the same way as the real life Fr Carton did (*cf.* Maher, 2001: 73–4). When asked if the whiskey caused any problems to his ulcer, he says: "The doctors tell you not to touch it, but if you did everything the doctors told you to do your life

---

5 Michael J. Toolan's article, "John McGahern: The Historian and the Pornographer" (*Canadian Journal of Irish Studies*, 7, 2 December 1981, pp. 39–55), while generally positive in his treatment of the novel, does point out some inadequacies: "A further cause for concern is the way McGahern is beginning to people his fictions with minor characters, often off-stage, whose portraits are either ill-focused or implausible. Thus, in *The Leavetaking*, Isobel's father is often difficult to accept, as is Isobel herself" (Toolan, 1981: 52). One could possibly add to that list Patrick's father and mother, who are not as successfully developed as they could have been.

wouldn't be worth living" (*L*, 166). Similarly, references to the Archbishop knowing all about his case draw more parallels with the real-life events and the way in which John Charles McQuaid intervened directly in McGahern's case to ensure his removal from his teaching position. It should be said that his dismissal caused McGahern much upset. He had difficulty writing for a number of years afterwards, which shows the extent of the emotional turmoil he endured. The line between fiction and autobiography is a very thin one and much time could be unprofitably spent on establishing links and determining what is fact and what is fiction.

I would like to deal briefly with the end of the novel when Patrick and Isobel decide to head back to England. Their last night in Ireland is spent making love. The narrative comes full circle as the narrator again notes that the "first constant was water and the gull's shadow floats again on the concrete, tea leaves are emptied again on the concrete, another day of our lives is almost ended, Ah love, let us be true to one another!" (*L*, 170). The novel ends with the lines:

> The odour of our lovemaking rises, redolent of slime and fish, and our very breathing seems an echo of the rise and fall of the sea as we drift to sleep; and I would pray for the boat of our sleep to reach its mooring, and see that morning lengthen to an evening of calm weather that comes through night and sleep again to morning after morning, until we meet the first death. (*L*, 171)

This is a fitting conclusion to a novel that seems to offer some hope for the redeeming power of love. All the loose ends are wonderfully brought together: gulls, shadows, memory, imagination and, of course, death. It is possibly the closest the novelist comes to supplying an optimistic vision of the world — he should not be judged on the type of vision he sketches, however, rather on how he moulds and shapes his canvas. Michael Toolan notes: "We must strive to re-enter a transcending sea of faith, whether that faith is in religion, or love, or literature." And he adds: "The last couple of pages of the novel are a marvellously judged cadence, a rich calling-to-mind, in the present tense, of the narrator's immediate reflections on the lovers' position at the beginning of the rest of their lives" (Toolan, 1981: 48). Terence Killeen (Killeen, 1991: 73) asserts that the very possibility of a hopeful future for the couple shows how far we have moved from the world of *The Barracks* and *The Dark*. There is a suspicion that memory and art may bring some harmony and healing to bear on existence. Certainly, there has been progression and evolution in that direction. The next novel we will discuss, *The Pornographer*, dashes those faint hopes and plunges us once more into a black philosophy of life hinted at, but not embraced, in *The Leavetaking*: "The true life was death in life. The sexual life was destruction; the sweet mouth, ruin. In my end was my beginning." (*L*, 156)

The Pornographer

It may have something to do with my background in French studies, but I have a real fondness for *The Pornographer*. It was well-received in France, where it was dubbed an "existential" novel. When this fact was mentioned to him, McGahern wisely said: "I'm not sure what that word [*existential*] means" (Ní Anluain, 2000: 151). I think I have at least some notion as to what would prompt commentators to see parallels between McGahern's work and that of an existentialist writer like Camus, for example. Denis Sampson mentions that many commentators noted similarities between *The Pornographer* and Camus's *L'Étranger*. In both instances, the main characters seem cold and unemotional. They are hedonistic and predatory in the sexual arena and they find it difficult to feign emotions they don't feel. Camus's Meursault is found guilty of

murdering an Arab by a French court which would have attached little enough importance to Arabs, mainly because he
showed no emotion at his mother's funeral. He is thus assumed to be a "monster". The sea, the sun, his girlfriend,
Marie's hair and the dresses she wears, the simple pleasures of
life are what motivate Camus's character. He has no religious
convictions and refuses to pretend to be moved when the
magistrate shows him the Crucifix and asks him does he believe that Jesus died for us. When Meursault replies in the
negative, the magistrate is amazed at his lack of feeling — even
the most hardened criminals broke down when he showed
them the Cross. Henceforth, he has the prisoner classified as
a man without any religious convictions and addresses him
subsequently as "Mr Anti-Christ". Meursault is the embodiment of all that "respectable" people find most frightening: he
will not conform, lie, simulate or dissimulate, react in the way
that is acceptable or normal. In brief, he will not play the social game. When Marie asks him if he loves her, he says "No".
Later, when she asks why he agreed to marry her if he didn't
love her, he says that she seemed to want it and he didn't
mind too much one way or the other. Meursault's apparent
indifference to people and events brings him close to the attitude of McGahern's pornographer. The book elicited all types
of varying reactions from readers. Fintan O'Toole considered
it a "brilliant novel", but brilliant in its complexity, "a complexity that has to be approached with the wry, rueful humour
that anyone who lives in Ireland has had to develop. Its fris-
sons and tensions were those of a fractured, dissolving place"
(O'Toole, 1990).[6]

This is an astute observation, because McGahern makes
much play on the role and function of the pornographer in
the course of the novel. He himself was the one whose

---

[6] This is O'Toole's *Irish Times* review of *Amongst Women*, in which he also
makes some comments about *The Pornographer*.

sisters were asked at a wedding if their brother was the "one who wrote the dirty book" (Ní Anluain, 2000: 144), referring of course to the banning of The Dark. By producing a novel which contains several passages of real pornography, perhaps McGahern was having a gentle dig at the Censorship Board and its supporters for what it had done to him in 1965. Maybe he was saying: "Now that's what real pornography reads like!" But McGahern's motivation was probably deeper than that. In an interview with Eileen Kennedy, he explained what he had set out to achieve in this novel: "I was just using pornography to show the absence of feeling, in the old technique of using shade to show the place of the sun" (Kennedy, 1984: 40). This seems a plausible contention, but it is not one that holds any water for Michael Toolan who, in his article already cited, traces the evolution of McGahern's writing up to, and including The Pornographer. His main thesis is that there is no sustained "advance from a bleak pessimism of mood towards a muted optimism, any intimation that life is an exhilarating gift" (Toolan, 1981: 39) in McGahern's writings. Many critics mistakenly felt that The Leavetaking marked a new commitment in McGahern to "the healing and transcendental power of love" (Toolan, 1981: 39).

Toolan maintains that there are two approaches adopted by McGahern — that of the historian and that of the pornographer. As a historian, he is both intimately involved in, and concerned about, the characters and events he presents, yet he has also the gift of detachment from those events:

> In McGahern's contrasting authorial stance (in evidence towards the end of The Dark and throughout The Pornographer), the fictional world the reader encounters is starved [by the author] of imagination, colour, or a living culture; it is characterized by inhumanity, selfishness, cynicism and betrayal. And those

betrayals, I fear, only echo the greater betrayal by the author of his readers.

Toolan now comes to the kernel of his argument:

> For while the lyrical/historian approach . . . had involved detachment with concern, here there is detachment without concern, without perspective. (Toolan, 1981: 40)

This analysis recognises that the writer is entitled to use inhuman means to present fully an inhuman world. But it is precisely the world vision that causes problems. By presenting himself as the detached, unconcerned chronicler of pornography, there is a danger that his less than discerning readers will not possess the insights to register their repulsion at such a world-view. Because, to write in such a detached manner about vital human experiences such as sex, always involves the danger of arousing and degrading readers, of not caring about what impact the writing might have on them. Toolan presents a more lofty vision of the role of the artist:

> At the most general, we turn to contemporary writers for rich, challenging insights into the way we have lived, are living, or should live — or in order to see how we may live more fully. We find none of this in McGahern's latest novel. (Toolan, 1981: 41)

Once more, I see the relevance of the critique but I don't fully agree with its accuracy in this instance. The nameless narrator of *The Pornographer*, for all that he is cold and exploitative, interested primarily in satisfying his sexual and material needs, does possess insights into his own character and experiences something akin to remorse for the suffering he has inflicted on hapless victims at the end of the novel. He is also kind to his dying aunt. In fact, there are two characters in the pornographer: the considerate loving person when he is dealing with people like his aunt and the cynical, permissive city predator who writes pornography and stalks The Metropole dance floor. The rural–urban divide is strong and helps to explain why he falls in love with Nurse Brady, herself the product of a rural background. When travelling back with her in a taxi to the nurses' home, an old sweet scent reaches his nostrils, that of freshly-cut hay (P, 173), a smell he will always associate with the nurse and his country roots.

The change of mood from the end of The Leavetaking to the beginning of The Pornographer has as much to do with a new experiment with style as with McGahern's vision of existence. We note that Camus does not judge Meursault harshly. He presents him in a detached manner that nevertheless betrays some sympathy for his plight. Flaubert's comment about how the novelist must "feel deeply and think clearly" (Maher, 2001: 80) is often quoted by McGahern in a way that shows the empathy he had with that sentiment. Everything has to do with style and, in a way, McGahern might find in Michael Toolan's criticism of The Pornographer a backhanded compliment. Because it is clear to me that his objective in The Pornographer was to compose a European novel set in Ireland. He was determined to examine in a totally non-judgemental and detached way areas of Irish society that have long been the source of controversy: namely, sex and religion. The descriptions of Dublin, a city whose young inhabitants have apparently broken free of old taboos and repression with regard to sexual behaviour, are in places quite vivid. That said, McGahern is still most at home when describing what Toolan described as "that little postage stamp of native soil in the west of Ireland which he knows so well, in pursuit of the profound and transcendental regionalism practised by, par excellence, William Faulkner" (Toolan, 1981: 53–4). The novelist will return to that other terrain with telling effect in Amongst Women.

The Pornographer begins with the central character going to the train station to collect his uncle, to whom he is very attached. The opening lines, as in *The Leavetaking*, capture the atmosphere effectively:

> I watched the sun cross and recross the carriages as the train came in between the pillars, lighting the grey roofs, and then hands began to draw down windows, doors flew open, and the first figures met the platform with a jolt, and started to run. (*P*, 9)

His uncle is the last passenger through the gate, carrying his raincoat on his arm in spite of the fine weather. "A wise man always carries his coat on a good day" (*P*, 9) is the explanation the narrator imagines his uncle will supply for this precaution. There is an ease in the way the two men interact that betrays a mutual respect — the narrator was raised by his aunt and her husband Cyril, along with his uncle, a bachelor, after the death of his parents. Over a bottle of stout and a sandwich, the conversation comes around to the "patient" and the nephew tells his uncle that things are not looking good at all. Her husband, Cyril, has not been to see her: "He's good for nothing anyhow" (*P*, 9), according to his brother-in-law. They take a taxi to the hospital and when they arrive in the ward, they see the patient and must pretend that they haven't yet spotted her: "It would have been easier to walk down that corridor if we hadn't to pretend that we didn't know that she'd seen us, imprisoned and awkward in the enforced deceit" (*P*, 12). They bring her a bottle of brandy — she finds it's the best way of killing the pain — and the visit takes on the form of all visits:

> Now that it was taking place it amounted to the nothing that was the rest of our life when it too was taking place. It would become part of our life again in the memory. In both the apprehension and the memory it

> was doomed to live far more vividly than in the taking
> place. (P, 13)

There is a deep truth to this sentiment which should strike a
chord with every reader. "Memory regained" is more vivid
than the actual "taking place" of any event. Events tend to
pass us by as they are being lived out and only assume real
significance when recalled *post facto*. The pornographer admits that he is "dead of heart" following the end of an affair
with a young woman with whom he was in love and who
jilted him. This understandably left him quite indifferent to
women in general. This indifference (the strongest character-
istic of Meursault's character) does not extend to his aunt,
however, to whom he is genuinely devoted. He does have
quite a black philosophy of life and yet it is hard to argue with
some of his insights:

> Our last conscious moment was the moment when
> our passing non-existence and our final one would
> marry. It seemed felicitous that our going out of life
> should be as similarly arranged as our coming in. (P, 13)

The narrative is interspersed with such observations that all
point to the circular nature of existence, which is a constant
preoccupation in McGahern's writings. One has only to think
of the short story "Wheels" in this regard. The son returns
home to visit his father and step-mother and realises that his
father's frailty puts him in the position of being the son's de-
pendant: "I knew the wheel: fathers become children to their
sons who repay the care they got when they were young, and
on the edge of dying the fathers become young again" (CS, 8).
The Pornographer contains a good deal of discussion of how
our lives are but a blur in the vast spaces of eternity. We are
born, live for a while and then return to oblivion:

> The womb and the grave. . . . The christening party
> becomes the funeral, the shudder that makes us flesh
> becomes the shudder that makes us meat. They say
> that it is the religious instinct that makes us seek the
> relationships and laws in things. And in between there
> is time and work, as passing time, and killing time, and
> lessening time that'd lessen anyway. (P, 30)

With such a fatalistic attitude, it does not come as too great a surprise that the narrator has endured hurt in his emotional life. It also partly explains why he writes pornography in his spare time. Michael Toolan argues that the pornographer could possibly be the development of Mahoney from *The Dark* (Toolan, 1981: 46), a plausible thesis. Certainly, we have the impression that there is a budding writer in Mahoney and it is not hard to see him as someone who became "dead of heart".

While in the company of his aunt and uncle he remains open and considerate because they have earned his trust. But as soon as he has dropped his uncle off at the train station after their hospital visit, the other side of the pornographer comes to the fore. He meets his publisher, Maloney, a *poète manqué* who has made his fortune from pornography. Trapped in a loveless marriage — his wife became pregnant when they were courting — he doesn't like to see his authors escaping from his sphere of influence. He is the one who attempts to define how his protégé should write: "'Above all, the imagination requires distance,' he declared. 'It can't function close up'" (P, 21). This is surprisingly close to the opinion expressed by many great writers. In the case of the writers of pornography, however, what Maloney means is that there should be no personal engagement whatever with the subject matter. Colonel Grimshaw and Mavis Carmichael, the two main actors in the pornographer's storyline, are sexual athletes and nothing else. There should be no need to develop their background or moral characters — all the readers want are the sordid details of their sexual activity. The narrator makes the mistake of using episodes from his own life in his writings. There is plenty of scope here, as can be gleaned from his escapades.

After his discussion with Maloney, he heads off to The Metropole, that famous ballroom frequented by many young Irish people during the 1950s and '60s. He describes it as a "racecourse" which abounded in "vulnerable flesh" (*P*, 31). On this fateful night he meets Josephine, a thirty-eight-year-old bank clerk, whom he describes as "a wonderful healthy animal" (*P*, 34) — the racecourse metaphor is thus maintained. They return to his flat and make love. She is almost a virgin — her membrane was partially penetrated a number of years previously.[7] Although outwardly pious and conservative, she becomes sexually the more aggressive as the relationship develops. She doesn't want him to use condoms ("It turns the whole thing into a kind of farce" (*P*, 56)) and not surprisingly ends up getting pregnant.

The pornographer, to his credit, admitted from the outset that he felt no love for Josephine and said that he wouldn't marry her after she had the child.[8] He had thought that marriage was the only option open to him originally until a conversation with a college friend, Peter White, a doctor, and his wife reveals other options. He wants to assume responsibility, to "take the blame for the whole business" (*P*, 112). Peter mentions the possibility of an abortion — which the narrator knows is not an option — or of having the child

---

[7] Her lover's lack of interest in any post-coital discussion is borne out by his absorption in the racing results.

[8] It is significant that Maloney feels that he should marry her, perhaps because that was the only path that he saw fit to follow when faced with the same dilemma in his own life. Although he likes to think of himself as a liberal, Maloney at times betrays a very strong streak of moral righteousness.

and giving it up for adoption. The fact that these alternatives are available to Irish people in the first instance is revealing of the culture swing in Ireland since the publication of *The Dark*.

I believe also that the fact that McGahern's second novel was banned and that *The Pornographer* wasn't — in spite of its containing quite lurid descriptions of oral and different types of depraved sex — is symptomatic of a burgeoning independence from Church interference in private and public affairs. Sex is no longer the taboo it was for Mahoney. Young people in this novel are openly engaged in permissive activity without any obvious signs of remorse. This is why I believe that Maloney's comment after the funeral of the pornographer's aunt is wide of the mark:

> "Look at today — isn't the whole country going round in its coffin! But show them a man and a woman making love — and worst of all enjoying it — and the streets are full of "Fathers of eleven", "Disgusted" and the rest of them. Haven't I been fighting it for the past several years, and giving hacks like you employment into the bargain." (*P*, 249)

The attitude he describes would have been largely confined to a mind-set and a set of principles that began to wane with the advent of the 1960s with its emphasis on sexual liberation, drugs and music. The dance halls became popular meeting places for young people anxious to experiment with sex and to live out some of the drama they were now seeing acted out by pop stars and in television dramas. Old habits die hard, however, and there was a strong conservative backbone in Ireland right up to and including the 1990s. The divorce and abortion referenda provided a battleground that was bitterly disputed between the liberal and conservative camps up until very recently. I mention these things to illustrate that the publication of *The Pornographer* coincided with a period of great upheaval and change in Ireland. The fact that

Josephine declares that she feels no guilt about the sexual relationship she enjoys with her partner shows a serious shift in the Irish mindset. Here we have sex divorced from religious significance, a real departure, particularly for the Irish female.

Let's return to Josephine for a moment. She is in many ways an unsympathetic and manipulative woman who knows full well the probable consequences of her actions. She wants her lover to marry her. On discovering she is pregnant her first suggestion is that they will have to get married. When that fails, after giving birth she insists on his coming over to London to meet her — she is staying with an Irish family, the Kavanaghs.[9] Josephine wants the pornographer to agree to see their child. Knowing the ruse she has in mind, he declines the offer and ends up being badly beaten up by Josephine's protector, Michael Kavanagh. Eileen Kennedy says of this episode: "The beating is the moment of grace for the narrator who hides from his assailant in the sheltered doorway of a church" (Kennedy, 1983: 124).

The differences between Josephine and the narrator are evident from the first time they make love. She feels liberated by the experience and states that it appears to be the most natural thing in the world. He, on the other hand, is looking for something deeper, almost mystical:

> Within her there was this instant of rest, the glory
> and the awe, that one was as close as ever man could
> be to the presence of the mystery, and live, the caged

---

[9] Initially she was staying with Jonathan, an elderly and wealthy publisher with whom she was friendly. When he proposed marriage to her, saying he would adopt the child and raise it as his own, she refused. She claimed to be shocked by his overtures! Jonathan then proceeded to move another woman into the house in her place.

bird in its moment of pure rest before it was about to
be loosed into blinding light. (*P*, 39)[10]

Meanwhile Josephine is crying: "This is what I needed. This-is-
what-I-need-ed." Her reaction prompts the conclusion from
the narrator: "We were more apart than before we had
come together" (*P*, 39). With such differing expectations, it is
no surprise that the relationship should fail. Still, the narrator
is happy to persevere with things long after his "dead heart"
has been revealed to Josephine. He begins to associate sex
with death. The following is his description of an orgasm:
"Death must sometimes come in the same way, the tension
leaving the body, in pain and not in this sweetness and pride,
but a last time, the circle completed" (*P*, 57). The circle is an
obsessive image in this novel. It brings the narrator back to
the farm bequeathed to him by his parents at the end of the
novel, where he hopes to live with Nurse Brady. This is an
appropriate moment to discuss the contrast between what
the pornographer feels about the two women:

> This body [the nurse's] was the shelter of the self.
> Like all walls and shelters it would age and break and
> let the enemy in. But holding it now was like holding
> glory, and having held once was to hold it — no mat-
> ter how broken and conquered — in glory still, and
> with the more terrible tenderness. (*P*, 177)

He doesn't try to encourage the attraction he feels for the
nurse until the situation with Josephine has been resolved. He
knows that he has fallen in love again but hopes that it won't

---

[10] Denis Sampson provides an excellent analysis of these lines: "This spiritual ecstasy, associated with the traditional Catholic image of the release of
the soul from the cage of the body, appears to be conditioned in part by
thoughts of the conundrum of time and eternity" (Sampson, 1993: 142). It
is a striking image to use and one whose underlying theological framework
would have been known to McGahern.

have the same unhappy consequences as his first experience of love. He sees his problems with Josephine as the opposite side of that particular coin. With her, he is the one that is being sought after:

> It seems we must be beaten twice, by the love that we inflict and then by the infliction of being loved, before we have the humility to look and take whatever agreeable plant that we have never seen before, because of it being all around our feet, and take it and watch it grow, choosing the lesser truth because it's all we'll ever know. (P, 219)

At times like these, the pornographer is not utterly reprehensible. He is as dispassionate about himself as he is about others. He has the ability also to see parallels of all sorts. On one occasion, as he goes to meet Josephine, he cannot avoid comparing this situation with his many visits to his aunt in hospital:

> And each evening as I went to meet her I did not think there was much difference (except in the quality of affection) from going in to see my aunt in the hospital . . . , except my male body in its cloth covering replaced the brandy bottle in its brown parcel. (P, 135)

Visiting his aunt brings Nurse Brady into his field of vision. His aunt spots the attraction immediately and often pokes fun at him about the nurse being "man-mad". When they finally do hit it off together, there is a poignant moment when he passes by the window of the ward where his aunt is suffering:

> I was going past that same window in a taxi, a young woman by my side, my hand on her warm breast. I shivered as I thought how one day my wheel would turn into her section, and I would lie beneath that win-

dow while a man and woman as we were now went past into the young excitement of a life that might seem without end in this light of the moon. (*P*, 172)

His relationship with the nurse is devoid of the callousness that characterises his liaison with Josephine because — at least this is what we are led to believe — she, like him, his aunt and uncle, all he holds most dear, is associated with the home farm to which he feels he must return in order to rediscover the purity of childhood. He thinks of the women in his aunt's ward who were giving birth to their own death while Josephine was preparing to bring a new life into the world in London: one circle ending and another beginning. He realises that his life is bringing him back to his starting point:

> All the doctrines that we had learned by heart and could not understand and fretted over became alarmingly clear. To find we had to lose: the road away became the road back. . . . All, all were travelling. Nobody would arrive. The adventure would never be over even when we were over. It would go on and on, even as it had gone on before it had been passed on to us. (*P*, 203)

There is a sense in which the pornographer believes himself to be powerless over the direction his life takes. He acknowledges that even if the nurse agrees to marry him and return to live in the country, his happiness is in no way guaranteed. But his announcement to Maloney, as they travel back to Dublin after burying his aunt, of his intention to return to live in the west indicates a serious step on the road to his achieving some sort of normality in his life. The visit to his uncle's house had confirmed him in his decision: "It was a big slated nineteenth-century farm house, five front windows and a solid hall door looking confidently down the road" (*P*, 233). This reassuring setting is sufficient reason for him to see that he belongs in a similar rural setting. He believes, rightly or wrongly, that he can rediscover some of the elements that make him a better person away from Dublin.

Karlheinz Schwartz notes: "In *The Pornographer* McGahern has created a character who, unlike his former characters, does not try to free himself from Irish restrictions but rather from human restrictions. In doing so, he finds hope in an unbiased acceptance of life" (Schwartz, 1983: 110). To better assess this analysis, we should point out that the narrator's emotion is such that he feels an urge to pray, even though he believes that his prayers cannot be answered.

The novel concludes by circling back to the first page of the book which described his uncle getting off the train in Dublin about a year previously with the air of a man who was uncomfortable to be out of his natural environment. That was "the beginning of the journey — if beginning it ever had — that had brought each to where we were, in the now and forever" (*P*, 252). There is once more the tantalising notion of time and eternity merging — we live somehow in the "now and forever". This means that events that occur, people who cross our paths, our passing moments on this earth have little significance in the greater scheme of things. Perhaps it is this sort of thought that makes some people consider *The Pornographer* an existential novel. Eileen Kennedy provides the following assessment: "The novel ends on an exultant note, in which the rain [which keep the wipers on Maloney's car busy] is a kind of baptism for the narrator" (Kennedy, 1983: 125). I do not read as much optimism into it myself, but neither would I go as far as to share Michael Toolan's robust assertion:

> The narrator characterises the experiences recorded in the book as a journey, but unfortunately for this reader at least that journey has been a meaningless one, and that judgement cannot be expunged by the contrived assertion of new knowledge and purpose

ascribed to the narrator at the book's close. (Toolan, 1981: 53)

I think I would lean more towards the assessment of Denis Sampson who sees that the journey travelled by the narrator has artistic as much as moral implications. He accuses himself openly of having caused suffering and pain. He reflects on the fact that he failed to notice the nurse one night when she was present in the same dance as himself. She tells him that he would have seen her had he been paying attention:

> By not attending, by thinking any one thing was as worth doing as any other, by sleeping with anyone who'd agree, I had been the cause of as much pain and confusion and evil as if I had actively set out to do it. I had not attended properly. (*P*, 251)

There is definite evidence in these lines of at least some moral regeneration, but I return to the point made by Denis Sampson with regard to the development being also, if not primarily, an artistic one: "The story he has to tell is the story of how he was reborn as a writer, transformed from the *artiste manqué*, the pornographer, into the narrator of the novel" (Sampson, 1993: 151). When he states that he wants to "follow the instinct for the true", he is laying down a marker in terms of his writing in the future. He is going to follow a different path from the one advocated by Maloney: "And be careful not to let life in. Life for art is about as healthy as fresh air is for a deep-sea diver" (*P*, 129). Life has to enter into his art if it is to assume any real meaning, any universal significance.

The Leavetaking and *The Pornographer* mark a significant development in McGahern's conception of the role of the artist. He has taken new material, especially in *The Pornographer*, and dealt with it in different ways. The grail of the perfect style, of the harmonious bonding of content and form, has not yet been achieved. It will have its crowning glory in *Amongst Women*, the culmination of years of refining his style and mining his material. Before we deal with that final period of his evolution, however, we will turn to the short stories, which offer us some useful insights into McGahern's vision of existence. Jürgen Kamm provides a good summary of the evolution of McGahern's fiction in the novels we have covered so far when he writes:

> If there is an innovative thrust in McGahern's writings it can be identified in his attempts to universalise Irish experience by imagination and intellectual vision. This blending is most successfully realized in *The Barracks*. . . . His later novels do not achieve a similar degree of artistic perfection because the vision becomes blurred and the writer finds it increasingly difficult to give satisfying expression to his philosophy. (Kamm, 1990: 187)

This assessment, which is totally valid for the novels up to and including *The Pornographer*, was written before the publication of *Amongst Women*, which saw McGahern returning to the familiar territory of his first novel with the additional advantage of a more mature craftsmanship. McGahern was learning in the tough school of human living. He internalised the experiences and out of them created his best book (from an artistic point of view, that is). *Amongst Women* is a point of arrival, of achievement, of universal significance within the cocoon of a dominated rural family in an almost claustrophobic rural community. The novelist, at the end of *The Pornographer*, returns to the country which he has subsequently never left in his fictional writing.

Chapter Three

Snapshots of Existence:
The Collected Stories

McGahern is considered a master of the short-story form. It suits his predilection for shaping, rewriting and restructuring. As he remarked in his Preface to the 1984 edition of *The Leavetaking*, it is most unusual for a writer to revisit a novel — the short story is more amenable to this type of exercise. His attitude to the short story is that it is not social in the same way as a novel is:

> I think the novel is a wonderful form, because I think it's the closest to society. And I mean — naturally one has to have self-respect, but I think the most profound thing is to respect other people, and since it is the most social of all the forms, including poetry and drama, in a way I think it actually is the most important form. The short story isn't social at all. It's just a small explosion, and in a way the whole world begins before the short story begins, and in a way a whole world takes place afterwards, which the reader imagines. And it generally makes one point and one point only, and has a very strict rhythm, and every word counts in it. (Louvel/Ménégaldo/Verley, 1995: 28)

The emphasis he places on rhythm and the importance of choosing the appropriate and properly weighted words, are skills which McGahern has perfected. He is good at placing the reader immediately at the heart of the subject, at using dialogue to advance the plot, at developing characters who are in some ways the mirror of their physical and cultural environments.

The Collected Stories were published in 1992 and bring together in slightly revised form his three previously published books of short stories: *Nightlines* (1970), *Getting Through* (1978) and *High Ground* (1985). There is a strange coherence to the collection, a type of interior structure that belies the fact that they belong to different stages in the author's development. It is true that the depiction of the Roscommon-Leitrim countryside and the tension of the families living there are more stark, perhaps even more resentful, in the earlier stories. For example, "Wheels", the first story in the collection, shows how the main character has fallen out with his father over his perceived lack of enthusiasm for the old man's suggestion that Rose, his second wife, and he move to Dublin. When the two finally get to speak in the fields, there is considerable bitterness:

> There was the dangerous drag to enter the emotion, to share and touch, the white lengths of beechwood about his boots and the veins swollen dark on the back of the old hands holding the sledge. With his sleeve he wiped away tears.
>
> "The one important thing I ever asked you couldn't even be bothered", he accused.
>
> "That's not true. When you wrote you wanted to move to Dublin I went round the auctioneers, sent you lists, looked at places."
>
> "And you said if I did get a place and moved that you wanted no room in it."
>
> "I want to live on my own. I didn't want you to come thinking differently." (*CS*, 8)

One senses the temptation the son feels to get closer to his father in his tears and to make peace with him. This is followed by a withdrawal of emotional sympathy as he suspects that he is being manipulated. The father, like many of the patriarchs in McGahern's fiction, wants to have things on his own terms or not at all. When the son suggests that it would have been inappropriate for him to interfere in a decision as to where his father and stepmother should live, he is told: "I'd give anything to get out of this dump" (*CS*, 9). The son, who has been living for some years in Dublin, thinks the countryside is "quiet and beautiful". The father replies:

> "Quiet as a graveyard . . . And stare at beauty every day and it'll turn sicker than stray vomit. The barracks shut now, a squad car in its place. Sometimes children come to the door with raffle tickets, that's all. But there's plenty of funerals." (*CS*, 9)

Here is pinpointed in a few images the depopulation of rural Ireland that began in the 1950s and has continued ever since. *That They May Face the Rising Sun* is based in a community very like the one described here, with the difference that the characters in the latest novel do not view their plight in such negative terms. Their relations with neighbours and friends, their work on the land and with their animals are, by and large, fulfilling for them.

The father in "Wheels" sees beauty as being "sicker than stray vomit", perhaps because he is in a constant struggle with nature through his work on the farm. He is the sick one but he does not realise it. The son marvels at how this man with the stinking sweat-band "had started my journey to nowhere" (*CS*, 6). He knows that he has been spared the task of looking after him in his old age by the arrival of Rose. His journeys home from the city give the son a sense of identity and rootedness. He knows that he has been shaped by the environment of his youth and that he can never completely escape from it. He looks forward to meeting his friend, Lightfoot, when he returns to Dublin, but he realises that he will be unable to recreate satisfactorily for the latter the full impact his visit home has had on him. He reflects on the "repetition of a life in the shape of a story that had as much reason to go on as to stop" (CS, 10). Liliane Louvel (2000: 68) maintains that this sentence refers back to the beginning of the story when the narrator overheard the account given by porters of a failed suicide attempt by a man who went out fishing beyond Islandbridge. The narrator remarks that "the story [was] too close to the likeness of my own life for comfort" (CS, 3). The absurdity of the branch breaking and the man surviving his self-destructive deed mirrors the narrator's futile attempts at making peace with his father.

There is an expected circular pattern in "Wheels" that is replicated in nearly all McGahern's work. His characters look back towards the past in an effort to understand what they have become — in order to make sense of their future. As he is travelling on the train to Dublin after his visit home, the narrator experiences moments from his past relived in the present:

> Through the windows the fields of stone walls, blue roofs of Carrick, Shannon river. Sing for them once First Communion Day *O River Shannon flowing and a four-leaved shamrock growing*, silver medal on the blue suit and the white ankle socks in new shoes. (CS, 10)

It is this experience of "memory regained" that causes him to reflect on the circular nature of existence and, more particularly, about art with its "vivid sections of the wheel we watched so slowly turn, impatient for the rich whole that never came but that all the preparations promised" (CS, 11).

The wheel trying to come full circle is a recurring symbol in McGahern. The individual stories of this collection could be described, in fact, as the "vivid sections of the wheel" that come together to form one large canvas depicting McGahern's vision of the world. Denis Sampson (2000: 25) observes that even if the disaffected narrator of "Wheels" is unable to believe in the existence of a "rich whole", this is merely a challenge to McGahern to find it, and to the reader to recognise it. This is precisely what he attempts to do in *The Collected Stories*, which provide us with a series of whirring snapshots of existence. When they are put together, they do not coalesce but they come close to the "rich whole". I argue that the perfect circle is never fully achievable in art any more than in life, but there are times when art can transcend the boundaries of time and place and achieve universality. This is the goal that McGahern sets himself as a writer.

We have considered the opening short story of the collection and have seen how it outlines some of McGahern's aesthetic ambitions. The last story, "The Country Funeral", takes many of the ideas found in "Wheels" but develops them in a more leisurely manner that gives the writer scope for character development and plot elaboration.

"The Country Funeral" is more a novella than a short story. It is thirty-five pages in length and it describes how three brothers, resident in Dublin, attend their uncle's funeral in the west of Ireland. Their journey down the country is at one and the same time geographical and mental. As young children they had spent their summers on their uncle's farm. It was a way for their mother to save money while giving her children the benefits of fresh country air. Philly is the most enthusiastic about the funeral. He works on the oil wells in Saudi Arabia and comes home for a few weeks every summer. He spends the days and most of the nights of his holidays in the pub, buying drink and pretending that his life is better than it is. His brother, Fonsie, is confined to a wheelchair and is harsh in his assessment of how Philly throws his money around and plays the big-shot. He is reluctant to attend the funeral of a man who, he believes, made them feel unwanted:

"He made us feel we were stealing bread out of his mouth" (CS, 389). Because of his infirmity, Fonsie believed that he was particularly at risk from his uncle: "The man wasn't civilized. I always felt if he got a chance he'd have put me in a bag with a stone and thrown me in a bog hole" (CS, 381–2). The third brother, John, a teacher, is the only one married. He is quiet-spoken and melancholy but is delighted to have an excuse to take a couple of days' leave from school. Before they depart, their mother gives an insightful appraisal of the people whom they will meet and why it is imperative that they attend:

> "If nobody went to poor Peter's funeral, God rest
> him, we'd be the talk of the countryside for years. . . .
> If I know nothing else in the world I know what
> they're like down there." (CS, 377)

Her advice does nothing to dull Philly's excitement. He sees the past through rose-tinted glasses and remembers the area around his uncle's farm with fondness: "the pictures of Gloria Bog that flooded his mind shut out the day and the room with amazing brightness and calm." (CS, 377) This reference to Gloria Bog is a throw-back to an earlier story in the collection, "The Recruiting Officer". Denis Sampson (2000: 29) makes the point that McGahern's changing perspective in relation to the countryside is evident in how the same area is referred to in a completely different light in the two stories. In the earlier one, the disillusioned teacher refers to "the empty waste of wheat-coloured sedge and stunted birch of the Gloria Bog" (CS, 107). It has none of the illuminating power with which Philly imbues it. In the later story, on the night they arrive for the wake, the bog assumes a luxuriance of which the earlier description was bereft:

> It was a clear moonlit night without a murmur of wind,
> and the acres of pale sedge were all lit up, giving back
> much of the light it was receiving, so that the places

> that were covered in heather melted into a soft black-
> ness and the scattered shadows of the small birches
> were soft and dark on the cold sedge. (*CS*, 393)

What had previously been "wasted" and "stunted" is now "lit
up" and "soft".

There is a similar evolution in the portrayal of the characters. The teacher in "The Recruiting Officer" ends his long day,
during which many images of his former life as a trainee Christian Brother are revived, by downing several whiskeys at the
Bridge Bar. This sequence appears destined to be repeated
every evening of his seemingly meaningless life. For Philly, however, the story ends with his decision to return to live on his
uncle's farm where he hopes to find fulfilment, happiness, perhaps even married bliss. The countryside has an almost thera-
peutic quality in this account that reminds us of the end of *The
Pornographer*. Philly may not discover what he is seeking and
yet there is something in the ambience and the pace of life in
the country that will, we suspect, suit his purposes. The peace
of the house during the wake has a spiritual quality that antici-
pates the scene in *That They May Face the Rising Sun* where
Ruttledge lays out Johnny's corpse. In death, Peter attains a
peace and a nobility that he had never known in life:

> In the upper room there was silence, the people
> there keeping vigil by the body where it lay in the
> stillness and awe of the last change; while in the lower
> room that life was being resurrected with more vivid-
> ness than it could ever have had in the long days and
> years it had been given. (*CS*, 392)

This wonderfully understated prose describes the Irish tendency to exaggerate the virtues of a dead person and to make
him into something he never was. The Rosary is recited, the
clocks silenced, the people drink stout and whiskey and eat
sandwiches. They recount tales in close circles, as though

anxious to assert through their physical proximity the fact that *they* at least are still alive. The rituals associated with death are always treated with the greatest delicacy by McGahern, as with his treatment of religious ceremonies. We sense how the Irish wake is designed primarily towards reassuring the living rather than mourning the dead. Alone in his uncle's house that night, Philly reflects on the life that has ended:

> He thought of Peter sitting alone here at night making the shapes of animals out of matchsticks, of those same hands now in a coffin before the high altar of Cootehall church. Tomorrow he'd lie in the earth on the top of Killeelan Hill. A man is born. He dies. Where he himself stood now on the path between those two points could not be known. He felt as much like the child that came each summer years ago to this bog from the city as the rough unfinished man he knew himself to be in the eyes of others, but feelings had nothing to do with it. He must be already well out past halfway. (*CS*, 396)

Life and death are intermingled in McGahern's writings; they are both taken seriously and delicately portrayed. Philly's is the sort of "epiphany" that occurs quite regularly in McGahern's stories. Philly has a good understanding of his shortcomings and of his mortality. It is probably at this moment that he makes the decision to buy the farm off his mother and to settle down there. He may be perceived by others and by himself as a "rough, unfinished man" but he still hopes that he can bring some order to his life in this setting that is closely linked with his youth and his memories. It is a fact that as we get older the images of childhood become more vivid and assume an increased importance.

Philly sees that he cannot continue indefinitely on the oil trail. His decision is a reasonable one. Fonsie is not so impressed, however. He is fonder of Philly than he cares to admit: "The burly block of exasperation would always come and go from the oilfields. Now he would go out to bloody Gloria Bog instead" (*CS*, 408). The two brothers argue a lot, but the strength of their differences betrays "the hidden closeness" (*CS*, 405). Philly sees himself being buried in the graveyard in Killeelan alongside his mother's family. What Fonsie will do with himself is another issue. Clearly, he needs the assistance of his family but it is doubtful whether he could endure living in a house that holds so many bad memories for him. Fonsie is more sceptical about the neighbours, the Cullens, and the other rural inhabitants. As he watches the coffin being carried to its resting place at the top of the hill, he is moved in a way that he finds uncomfortable:

> He found the coffin and the small band of toiling mourners unbearably moving as it made its low stumbling climb up to the hill, and this deepened further his irritation and the sense of complete uselessness. (*CS*, 400)

The characters come to life through sentences like this one, as Fonsie gives vent to his resentfulness at being confined to a wheelchair.[1] He hates to be a burden on his mother and

---

[1] James Whyte provides a good analysis of how the reader is given the individual viewpoints of each of the three brothers: "The narrative method, developed in *High Ground* and perfected in *Amongst Women*, is ideally suited to this task. It is a third-person, omniscient and thoroughly objective narration, for the most part composed of a mixture of description and dialogue. . . . Using this method, the author manages to allow each of the characters (especially the three brothers) his own separate existence and his own point of view with a tact equal to that of the rural community working within the system of manners governing the funeral" (Whyte, 2002: 122). In addition, he draws parallels between "The Country Funeral" and Joyce's "The Dark", both of which are the longest stories and come at the end of *The Collected Stories* and *Dubliners*. They also deal with a western movement and focus on a social event that brings two generations together. And then there is, of course, the theme of death that is common to both (Whyte, 2002: 119).

family and can only hit out at his "uselessness" by verbally assaulting Philly.

The story, as well as providing us with characters who are credible and who etch themselves on our consciousness, also contains beautiful descriptions of landscape. McGahern rounds it off beautifully as the three sons go home to their mother who declares: "I followed it all on the clock. . . . I knew the Mass for Peter was starting at eleven. . . . At twenty past twelve I could see the coffin going through the cattle gate at the foot of Killeelan" (CS, 408). She, like Philly, has a strong sense of place, custom and ritual. She experienced the funeral almost as fully as if she had been there herself.

The last lines of the story, which also close the collection, bring us full circle to that "rich whole" that was so eagerly sought in "Wheels". We feel as if finality has been achieved, even if it is the finality of death:

> "Anyhow, we buried poor Peter," Philly said, as if it
> was at last a fact. (CS, 408)

This may not rival in intensity the catharsis experienced by Gabriel at the end of "The Dead":

> His soul swooned slowly as he heard the snow falling
> faintly through the universe and faintly falling, like the
> descent of their last end, upon all the living and the
> dead. (Joyce, 1996: 256)

That said, the conclusion of "The Country Funeral" is appropriate for the type of people it is describing. Philly does not possess any of the cultural sophistication and educational training of Gabriel and so does not have the ability to express his feelings in such an eloquent manner. But he knows that he has been changed by his trip to the West and that his life will never be quite the same again. There is finality in his pronouncement of a fact (they buried their uncle) that has been hard won and the reader feels that the wheel has come full circle — well, almost — since the first story in the collection.

I will now deal with some of the main themes of the collection: doomed relationships, family tensions/social commentary, memory regained, to show how the collection defines McGahern's approach to the art of fiction. These themes are basic elements in his fiction, both novels and short stories.

Doomed Relationships

We have seen in the earlier novels evidence of relationships between men and women that are doomed to fail. There is often a tendency to associate sex and death (particularly in *The Pornographer*), which is quite a dark parallel to draw. Sinclair, in "Why We're Here", is reported to have been seen outside Amiens Street with an empty shopping bag — a gesture that will be repeated by Michael, who finds himself outside a Tesco's supermarket in "A Slip-up" — looking "shook" (*CS*, 13). Sinclair converted to Catholicism for the love of a woman: "*It was no rush of faith, let me tell you good sir, that led to my conversion. I was dragged into your Holy Roman Catholic Apostolic Church by my male member*" (*CS*, 14; italics are McGahern's). This is the situation (though it is not described in such colourful language!) that also confronts William Kirkwood ("The Conversion of William Kirkwood") whose conversion is not initially prompted by the love of a Catholic woman. However, after becoming a Catholic, he is more accepted by the rural community, a development that allows him to meet and become engaged to Miss Kennedy. The impending marriage means that Annie May and her illegitimate daughter, Lucy, who have lived and worked in the Kirkwood household for years, will have to leave. So, at what should have been a most happy period in his life, Kirkwood feels the weight of his responsibility towards two people to whom he had grown very attached:

> He had many things to think about, and not least
> among them was this: whether there was any way his
> marriage could take place without bringing suffering
> on two people who had been a great part of his life,
> who had done nothing themselves to deserve being
> driven out into a world they were hardly prepared
> for. (*CS*, 349)

There is a sense in which marriage and sex cause more problems than they solve for McGahern's characters. Religion and sex are too inextricably mixed for people to adopt a relaxed attitude to their relationships. Even when characters escape the restrictive confines of their rural background and go to Dublin, where they have the freedom to experiment with sex, they don't seem capable of mature relationships and they remain fundamentally unhappy. "Coming into his Kingdom" describes how a young boy learns the facts of life and becomes suddenly aware of the sordid abuse that his father has been inflicting on him since the death of his mother:

> His father had slept with his mother and done that to
> her, the same father that slept with him now in the
> big bed with the broken brass bells and rubbed his
> belly at night, saying, "That's what's good for you,
> Stevie. Isn't that what you like, Stevie?" (*CS*, 21)

Sex is associated here with abuse, not love. Indeed, love and sex seldom unite in McGahern's work. The description above is similar to what happens young Mahoney in *The Dark*. We know how stunted Mahoney's sexuality became as a result of his father's abuse — he wasn't able to summon up the courage to go to the student dance in UCG and, although grown to manhood, he hadn't passed the stage of merely fantasising about women.

It would not be too outlandish to surmise that many of the men in *The Collected Stories* have endured similar torture from abusive fathers during their youth and that, as a result, they find it difficult to relate meaningfully to women. The story that best exemplifies this discomfort is "My Love, My Umbrella". The male character in this narrative becomes accustomed to having sex with his partner as she holds aloft an umbrella to shelter them from the falling rain. They met for the first time in a setting that would not inspire confidence as to the future of their relationship. One Sunday afternoon, their paths crossed as they stood listening to a band playing at the back of the public lavatory on Burgh Quay — not very auspicious surrounds! The words of the song the band were playing went like this: *Some day he'll come along / The man I love / And he'll be big and strong / The man I love.* The man she meets in reality does not conform to the description in the song: he is not "big and strong". He is, however, driven by desire on seeing a woman whose sensuality attracts him: "the solidity at the bones of the hips gave promise of a rich seed-bed" (*CS*, 65). They exchange a few meaningless sentences over drinks and eavesdrop on the drunken conversation of a poet which frees them from the onus of having to talk to one another. When they exit the pub, the heavy raindrops falling on the street remind him "of blackened spikes on the brass candle-shrine which hold the penny candles before the altar" (*CS*, 67). The image is appropriate, as soon he will feast on the altar of her body as she holds aloft the umbrella that is a symbol, in the opinion of Dominique Dubois, of: "a timorous refusal of any form of fecundity, be it material or spiritual as well as escapism. It is therefore a fit image to associate with someone who, throughout the story, has tried to escape his responsibility by having his girlfriend hold his umbrella for him and who has conscientiously spilled his seed on the ground" (Dubois, 2000: 58).

The couple repeat this ritual without there being any deepening of understanding between them. The relationship, based on sex, inevitably comes to an end. This is precipitated by the inappropriate stories they relate to one another. She

tells him about how, as an adolescent, she provoked a bachelor farmer with her body and then threatened to tell her father when, aroused, he went to grab her. This shows a
ruthless streak and an awareness of her power to seduce. He
relates the contents of an article he has read in a newspaper
about how two men in London assaulted each other with
umbrellas. He finds the judge's assertion that an umbrella was
a "dangerous weapon" amusing, especially in light of the use
to which they put his. She takes exception to his story and he
finds hers cruel.

One night, when it is not raining, she refuses to hold the
umbrella and he is annoyed. They begin to drift apart and the
break comes when she says that they are not suited and that
she thinks they should not see each other any more. It is
nearly always the woman who initiates the break in McGahern's stories and the man, who took his partner for granted,
finds it difficult to live with the pain of separation:

> Little by little my life had fallen into her keeping, it
> was only in loss I had come to know it, life without
> her, the pain of the loss of my own life without the
> oblivion the dead have, all longing changed to die out
> of my own life on her lips, in her thighs, since it was
> only through her it lived. (CS, 72)

The whole relationship has a touch of the absurd about it.
The woman is right to feel demeaned at appearing to be nothing other than an extension of the man's umbrella. The talk of
marriage seems ludicrous in light of the fact that they know
virtually nothing about each other outside of sexual intimacy.
The man's pain at the thought of his former lover being in the
embrace of another is so intense that he says that if he had
the power, he would "have made all casual sex a capital of-
fence" (CS, 73). He cuts a sad picture at the end of the story
as he continually takes the bus out to the place where they
had made "love", under the trees. Love and death are once

more intertwined: "Through my love it was the experience of my own future death I was passing through, for the life of the desperate equals the anxiety of death" (CS, 74). McGahern is no optimist when it comes to his portrayal of sex.

"Peaches" develops the theme of incommunicability further in a narrative that traces the experiences of an Irishman and a Scandinavian woman living in exile in post-Franco Spain. Both are writers but he has lost all zest for work and prefers to find solace for his professional frustration in a haze of alcohol. His partner's nagging about the fact that he has done no work for more than a year and that he doesn't look after her properly leave him feeling impotent. The smell of the stinking carcass of a dead shark on the beach penetrates their house and is a daily reminder of the man's artistic and physical decay. The foreign setting does not brighten the dark descriptions of relationships in the collection. McGahern's theory would appear to be that people are the same no matter where they go. Certainly the man in this story has many distinctive Irish traits. He remembers with some nostalgia the day of their wedding:

> A man is born and marries and dies, it'd be the toll of the second bell, one more to come; and there'd be no ceremonies, no ring, no gold or silver, no friends, no common culture or tongue: they'd offered each other only themselves. (CS, 82)

There is something lacking in this minimalist ceremony, a lack that characterises their relationship as a whole. Even when they make love, they seem miles apart. When she reaches orgasm, she does so "with a blind word in her own language" (CS, 87) and he feels that "their pleasures could hardly have happened more separately if they had been on opposite ends of the beach" (CS, 87). Nevertheless, they stay together even though their proximity is bringing them more pain than joy.

Realising that they are not making much progress, she suggests that they could go and see an analyst. His reaction is revealing: "If he had to go to an analyst he would return to the Catholic Church and go to confession, which would at least be cheaper" (CS, 87–8). The cultural barriers are ones from which they cannot escape. He remembers his Catholic formation and is incapable of changing sufficiently in order to become the sort of man his wife needs: strong, decisive, passionate.

The gulf between them becomes very wide when he fails to act decisively on the occasion when the local magistrate insists they accompany him to his villa where he shows them his peaches. He lets it be known unambiguously that he has designs on the woman and he proceeds to shove peaches into the breast pocket of her blue dress. He is boastful about his peaches and his plentiful supply of water, both symbols of fertility and potency, which provides a strong contrast with the couple's house where there is always a scarcity of water. The story ends with them having to leave the area because to stay would mean putting the woman at risk. She is not happy that her husband did not come to her aid when she was being subjected to humiliation and rejects his excuse that if he had hit the magistrate and ended up in a Spanish jail it wouldn't have done their cause any good:

> "You never give me any support. You know how awful it is to be married to a weak man. If I was married to a strong man like my father it would be different." (CS, 99)

"All Sorts of Impossible Things" tells how the shape of James Sharkey's life is sealed when, conscious of his impending baldness, he presses his girlfriend, Cathleen O'Neill, for an answer to his marriage proposal: "Anxiety exasperated desire to a passion, the passion to secure his life as he felt it slip away, to moor it to the woman he loved" (*CS*, 137). Unhappy at being cornered in this manner, the young woman will not give James a "Yes" or a "No". He takes this as a refusal and steels himself to turn away. He takes a few steps and looks back, hoping she will be facing in his direction, but she has her back turned to him: "As she passed through the gate he felt a tearing that broke as an inaudible cry" (*CS*, 138). From that moment on, James is never seen in public without his brown hat. The local parish priest is faced with a dilemma when James, a national school teacher who is expected to be a pillar of society, refuses to appear in church without this hat. The priest manages to find a compromise by allowing James to stay in the porch where he can look after the collection table. The brown hat is the symbol of James' refusal to allow others share in the humiliation he feels over his baldness. It is also a sign of the loneliness and despair that are his lot in life.

He gets enjoyment from going out coursing with his friend, Tom Lennon, an agricultural inspector who needs to pass exams in order to be made permanent. Tom suffers from a heart complaint and dies on the morning he is due to sit the exams. James remembers how his friend had asked him to give him a haircut the night before. As he embarked on the task, James felt moved as the black hair began to fall on the towel: "he felt for the first time ever a mad desire to remove his hat and stand bareheaded in the room, as if for the first time in years he felt himself in the presence of something sacred" (*CS*, 142–3). After the funeral, the same longing to throw away his hat takes hold of the teacher and he has the fleeting desire to find a girl and go to the sea with her as he had done with Cathleen O'Neill. But the last lines of the story show the temporary nature of such plans:[2]

---

2 The next story in the collection, "Faith, Hope and Charity" shows James Sharkey to be still wearing his brown hat.

> And until he calmed, and went into the house, his
> mind raced with desire for all sorts of such impossible
> things. (CS, 145)

The pattern of failed love affairs continues throughout the collection. The widowed teacher in "The Stoat" turns his back on Miss McCabe when he discovers that she has heart problems; when Kate O'Mara issues a request (that is also a test) to the narrator in "Doorways" that he stay with her rather than travel to Sligo, his refusal heralds the end of their relationship; "Parachutes" opens with the ending of a relationship that leaves a young man distraught and disoriented on a street in Dublin; in "A Ballad", O'Reilly tries in vain to evade his responsibilities towards his girlfriend whom he has made pregnant but ends up (most unusually for a McGahern story) happily married to her. "Like All Other Men" relates how, after a night of passion, a nurse tells the man with whom she has slept that she is joining the Medical Missionaries. Once more, a jilted lover finds himself alone with his thoughts in the anonymous city of Dublin:

> The river out beyond the Custom House, the straight
> quays, seemed to stretch out in the emptiness after
> she had gone. In my end is my beginning, he recalled.
> In my beginning is my end, his and hers, mine and
> thine. It seemed to stretch out, complete as the emp-
> tiness, endless as a wedding ring. (CS, 280)

"Eddie Mac" relates how a former football hero, whose powers of seduction are waning, embarks on an affair with Annie May.[3] On discovering she is pregnant, he flees to England with money secured from selling some of the Kirkwoods' livestock.

---

[3] This is the same woman who will be evicted along with her daughter in "The Conversion of William Kirkwood".

Disappointment, deception, lack of understanding, guilt and pain are some of the elements that recur most frequently in McGahern's short stories that deal with love. It is well summed up in the following lines from "Sierra Leone":

> Did we know one another outside the carnal pleasures we shared, and were we prepared to spend our lives together in the good or nightmare they might bring? It was growing clear that she wasn't sure of me and that I wasn't sure. (*CS*, 323)

There is consistency in the lack of success men and women encounter in finding a suitable partner. There is a fatalism evident in the doomed nature of human love. In spite of this distrust, however, couples still cling on desperately to the hope that they might one day shed the shackles of their past and know the exhilaration of a *grand amour*. For McGahern, it is a type of Holy Grail that always eludes them.

Family Tensions and Social Commentary

We know that the family is a core element in McGahern's philosophy of life. If unmarried couples are usually unhappy and dissatisfied with life, their married counterparts do not usually enjoy much more success. This may be because of how the two sexes in Ireland tended to be segregated for many social rituals during the 1940s and 50s. This, and many other factors, led to an incomprehension of the partner's needs and aspirations that didn't dissipate, even after many years of marriage. However, the family has a life of its own outside of the relationship between the mother and father. In an interview with James Whyte, McGahern outlined the importance of the family in Irish life: "The closest we have to a society in Ireland is the family." He went on to say that Irish society was, in fact, "made up of thousands of little republics called families" (Whyte,

2002: 136). We have seen the tensions that characterise life in these "republics" in McGahern's first four novels.

In keeping with the theory of the short story being like a "small explosion", this genre provides the author with a good opportunity to explore the stresses that occur in many families. The most common manifestation of tension is that between father and son, a tension that is very clear in "Wheels". However, it undoubtedly gets its best depiction in "Korea", a short story that was adapted into a successful film by Cathal Black. The story is only five pages long and yet it manages to unveil a tremendous tension. It begins with the son questioning his father about an execution he witnessed in Mountjoy, where he was imprisoned during the War of Independence. The image of the executed boy's buttons being thrown in the air by the impact of the bullets left an indelible mark on the father. Years afterwards, during his honeymoon, he and his wife go for a walk on the hill of Howth where the sight of the furze pods bursting rekindles memories of the execution and ruins his enjoyment of the day. A widower now for a number of years, the father is disillusioned with the Ireland that has emerged from his armed struggle. He has difficulty eking out a living from fishing eels on the lake and it looks likely that even that precarious livelihood will be lost with the imposition of a fishing licence. He understandably feels frustrated at the current state of affairs:

> "And the most I think is that if I'd conducted my own wars, and let the fool of a country fend for itself, I'd be much better off today." (*CS*, 58)

He dislikes having to talk about the war and the son reckons he only agrees to having the discussion with him because it is their last summer together before he is due to move away from home to make his way in the world. The father encourages him to go to America, the land of opportunity, and even offers to come up with the fare. He wonders about this sudden generous gesture until he overhears a conversation between his father and a cattle-dealer, Farrell, during which mention is made of the Moran family, whose son, Luke, was killed in the American army in Korea. Apparently, the Morans received a handsome payment after the death of Luke. The narrator is horrified at discovering his own father's motives in wanting to send him to America:

> The shock I felt was the shock I was to feel later when I made some social blunder, the splintering of a self-esteem and the need to crawl into a lavatory to think. (*CS*, 57)

At that moment, the young man knows that his life will never be the same again: "my youth had ended" (*CS*, 57). In his refuge, the lavatory, there are boxes of crawling worms and a "smell of piss and shit", which are a mirror of how the young man is feeling.[4] (In Black's film, the box of worms is changed into the eels in their net, which is a powerful image.) The effect of the revelation is to harden the young man against the world, and particularly against the man with whom he has spent his life up until that point. There is, however, no evidence of bitterness in the concluding lines of the story, but rather a realisation that he needs to be prepared to kill his father in order to survive:

> I'd never felt so close to him before, not even when he carried me on his shoulders above the laughing crowd to the Final. Each move he made I watched as closely as if I too had to prepare myself to murder. (*CS*, 58)

---

[4] James Whyte offers this assessment: "The effect is psychic death and an initiation into a new and terrible world, very different from that of his youthful naivety" (Whyte, 2002: 160).

There is a sense in which this undercurrent of violence fore-shadows the relationship between Moran and his two sons in *Amongst Women*. The veterans of the War of Independence are trained killers who continue their guerrilla campaigns in the home long after the war has ended. Closeness to the fa-ther does not dissipate an awareness of the danger of letting your defences drop. This story is an example of all that is best in McGahern's short stories. There is not a single word that could be removed without damaging the text. The con-versations have a telepathic quality and an authenticity that are remarkable. In the space of five pages, we get inside the minds of the two protagonists and we can see what makes them tick.

A brief look at two more stories will show a similar treatment of family tensions. "Gold Watch" depicts a soured relationship between a son and his father. The father is re-sentful at the opportunity that has been afforded to his off-spring to attend university. He dislikes the loss of power he once wielded and is annoyed at not being consulted about his son's engagement to be married. When the couple go to visit the father and step-mother, Rose, the young man is asked the age of his intended and is subjected to disbelief when he re-plies that she is the same age as himself. The only time there is some harmony is when father and son work side by side at the hay. The vigorous physical activity renders conversation unnecessary as the two are joined in their rush to complete the work before there is any break in the weather:

> Each cloud that drifted into the blue above us we watched as apprehensively across the sky as if it were an enemy ship, and we seemed as tired at the end of every day as we were before we had the machines, eating late in silence, waking from listless watching of the television only when the weather forecast showed; and afterwards it was an effort to drag feet

to our rooms where the bed lit with moonlight showed like heaven, and sleep was as instant as it was dreamless. (CS, 217–8)

When he travels down to help with the hay the following year, however, he is disappointed to discover that all the meadows have been cut and saved. His father had decided that it was too much work for himself and Rose to look after the winter feeding and so had let the meadows. He is aware of the enjoyment his son got from working in the fields and this was an opportunity to cause him pain. The gold watch mentioned in the title of the story is associated with power[5] — it has been handed down from father to son for generations. The son wants to possess it for that reason — the watch has not functioned properly for years — and offers the father an expensive replacement that he bought in duty free. The exasperation felt by the old man is evident as he openly dips the gift into a corrosive substance he uses to spray the potatoes. The son's hopes of a reconciliation are illusory because the older man is not capable of any gestures of appeasement:

It was a perfect moonlit night, the empty fields and beech trees and walls in clear yellow outline. The night seemed so full of serenity that it brought the very ache of longing for all of life to reflect its moonlit calm, but I knew too well it neither was nor could be. It was a dream of death. (CS, 224)

---

[5] Denis Sampson observes: "The son seems to realise that the ritual of passing on the watch is a civilised way of recognising that power is passing to a new generation, that the older generation must yield to the younger and that it would be a sign that the father supported or even blessed his independence and power" (Sampson, 1993: 185). There is little hope of such a concession from a man who wants to hold on to power, not to relinquish it. It is hard to disagree with Sampson's assessment that the watch, any watch, is a reminder to the father of his mortality, which explains his frantic efforts to destroy the replacement watch his son buys him.

Time is a constant preoccupation in the story. The father complains that Jimmy never rings the bell for the Angelus at the correct time: "Only in Ireland is there right time and wrong time" (CS, 219). The son loved to watch the second hand complete the circle of the gold watch when he was young. As he matures, he sees how, with the passing of the years, images of youth are restored with a vividness he had not appreciated at the time of their happening: "How clearly everything sang now set free by the distance of the years, with what heaviness the actual scenes and days had weighed" (CS, 219). The ending is not conclusive but there is no reason why it should be. The relationship between father and son is poisoned in the same way as happens to the new watch:

> And when I finally lowered the watch back down into the poison, I did it so carefully that no ripple or splash disturbed the quiet, and time, hardly surprisingly, was still running; time that did not have to run to any con-clusion. (CS, 225)

"Oldfashioned" dramatises the conflict between a Garda sergeant and his son over what is perceived as the way in which a local Protestant couple, the Sinclairs, exercise an un-healthy influence on the young boy. The Sinclairs are a thinly disguised representation of the Moroneys, the Protestant family that allowed McGahern full access to their library when he was young. Prejudice towards the British and an ill-informed distrust of their motives prompt a rift between the Sinclairs and the Garda sergeant. The boy expresses an inter-est in joining the British army and when Colonel Sinclair comes to discuss the possibility of such a choice, he is met with a blank refusal. The sergeant's character allows no room for compromise:

> He was not a man to look for any abstraction in the sparrow's fall. If that small disturbance of the air was

to earn a moment's attention, he would want to know at once what effect it would have on him or that larger version of himself that he was fond of referring to as "my family". By the time the Colonel had finished he was speechless with rage. (*CS*, 260)

Echoes of Moran in *Amongst Women* are evident in the concept of family being an extension of the father, the possessive pronoun "my" indicating ownership. As a veteran of the War of Independence, the sergeant is not going to allow his son join the "enemy" forces. The humdrum nature of life in the barracks, devoid of any intellectual or cultural stimulation, is a far cry from the sophistication of the Sinclair house. There can be no doubt as to where the boy would prefer to spend his time. Having lost their son in the War, the Sinclairs develop a great fondness for this child who shows intelligence and an ability to please. Their motivation in agreeing to speak to his father about becoming an officer in the British army is predicated on their appreciation of the fact that such a career would open up all sorts of educational and professional advantages to him. But the father is having none of it. The son is forbidden to visit the Sinclairs and they are once more made feel the pain of loss. Johnny, as the child is called, never really becomes reconciled to his father after this incident. When he gains a scholarship to university, he receives no praise: "You'll be like the rest of the country — educated away beyond your intelligence" (*CS*, 268). There is in this reaction another foretaste of Moran in *Amongst Women*.

By depicting family tensions, the stories are, in essence, also providing social commentary. In "Oldfashioned", there is a clear ironical parallel between the reaction to Johnny's work as a documentary filmmaker — his films are said to deal with "the darker sides of Irish life" (*CS*, 268) — and the reception McGahern's fiction elicited down the years:

> As they [the documentaries] were controversial, they
> won him a sort of fame: some thought they were se-
> rious, well made, and compulsive viewing, bringing
> things to light that were in bad need of light; but oth-
> ers maintained that they were humourless, morbid,
> and restricted to a narrow view that was more re-
> vealing of private obsessions than any truths about life
> or Irish life in general. (*CS*, 268–9)

When he returns to do a documentary about the village
in which he grew up, he notes the significant changes that
have occurred in the decades since he departed. Emigration,
which has devastated the countryside, now seems to have
subsided. There is more prosperity: "Most houses have a car
and colour television" (*CS*, 269). One no longer sees horses
and carts and only the rare bicycle. In addition, educational
opportunities are far more commonplace. Where once people aspired to travel to America or Britain, now they tend to
head as far as a "bursting Dublin" (*CS*, 269). There have been
changes also in religious practice:

> . . . the priest now faces the people, acknowledging
> that they are the mystery. He is a young priest and
> tells them that God is on their side and wants them
> to want children, bungalow bliss, a car, and colour
> television. (*CS*, 269)

There is no more pulpit-thumping, no emphasising of the sinfulness and fallen state of human beings. We hear that the
priest "plays the guitar and sings at local hotels where he is a
hit with the tourists" (*CS*, 270) and that he seldom wears
clerical garb. There has been a power shift from the clergy to
the political class and the clinic has replaced the presbytery in
terms of importance: "They come to look for grants, to try
to get drunken driving convictions squashed, to get free
medical cards, sickness benefit" (*CS*, 270). The Protestants

have all but disappeared and the general impression one gets is that rural Ireland has happily entered the modern world.

Johnny thinks to himself that all the people who had interested him are dead and that he will never successfully capture the society of his youth in the episode he plans to record for the series called *My Own Place*. There will be no people in the film, just images and the voice of the narrator. In the end, it appears that this will be sufficient to describe the changes that have taken place in the area:

> The camera panned slowly away from the narrator to the house, and continued along the railings that had long lost their second whiteness, whirring steadily on the silence as it took in only what was in front of it . . . lingering on the bright rain of cherries on the tramped grass beneath the trees, the flaked white paint of the paddock railing, the Iron Mountains smoky and blue as they stretched into the North against the rim of the sky. (*CS*, 271)

"High Ground" makes many of the same points as "Old-fashioned", but without employing the journalistic tone that jarringly intrudes at the end of the latter. In this instance, a young teacher comes back to his native village to attend a Building Fund Dance for the Christian Brothers' school of which he is a past pupil. During his stay, he is approached by Senator Reegan, who tries to persuade him to take up a position in the local national school — he has recently graduated from the teacher training college. Were he to accept, it would mean replacing Master Leddy who had taught him years previously. Reegan once more displays the power that has been assumed by the politicians at the expense of the clergy when he states his intention to have Leddy replaced as soon as possible:

> "Listen. There are many people who feel the same way as I do. If I go to the Canon [the School Manager] in the name of all those people and say that you're willing to take the job, the job is yours. Even if he didn't want to, he'd have no choice but to appoint you. . . ." (CS, 309)

The senator explains that the school is a shambles and that he cannot run the risk of his sons not getting a proper education. A few evenings prior to this encounter with Reegan, Moran, as the young man is called, had called in to see the Master at his home. After exchanging a few pleasantries, he is quickly ushered out the door and up the town — the Master has a thirst on him. It is Leddy's habit to go drinking every night, a fact that has not gone unnoticed in the village. This has clearly detracted from his performance in the classroom. Reegan is anxious for matters to be expedited with haste because, if the situation is allowed to develop further, it might be impossible to retrieve it. Moran feels guilty at the repercussions his appointment would have on his former mentor and yet he is aware that there is a logic to what Reegan has in mind.

As he goes out to the well late that night to get some water for the morning, he hears voices emanating from Ryan's Bar where a group is availing of after-hours drinking. The Master is holding forth in his customary fashion; he is a genial man, a harmless drunk who finds it easy to shine in this entourage made up of tradesmen and local farm workers, nearly all of whom he has taught. He knows how to ingratiate himself with these men:

> "Well, the people with the brains mostly stayed here. They had to. They had no choice. They didn't go to the cities. So the brains was passed on to the next generation. Then there's the trees. There's the water. And we're very high up here. We're practically at the source of the Shannon. If I had to pick on one thing

> more than another, I'd put it down to that. I'd attrib-
> ute it to the high ground." (*CS*, 315)

This is the type of social commentary that chronicles
some essential aspects of Irish life as well as anticipating the
changes that began to take hold of rural Ireland as early as
the 1960s. McGahern's feel for the small rural communities of
Roscommon and Leitrim is palpable in "High Ground". Leddy
is an identifiably local character with no aspirations towards
self-promotion. He is ignorant of the machinations of Reegan
and the other parents of children in his school and lives in a
type of time warp. He has charm in abundance, but no self-
discipline — how many men like him can be found scattered
across the country even today? However, there is a sense in
which they are a dying breed in a society that has embraced
technological innovation and material prosperity in the last
few decades. Sentiment no longer influences decisions as it
did in the 1940s and 1950s.

"Parachutes", with its Dublin setting, relates once more
the sad ending of a relationship. But it also provides us with
an insight into the drinking classes of the country's capital.
The ambience is significantly different to that found in "High
Ground", in part because of the urban–rural divide that pro-
motes different social value systems. Thus, in "Parachutes", a
couple like the Mulveys can go drinking together, something
that would only happen on rare occasions in the country —
Master Leddy's wife does not accompany him to the pub, for
example, nor are there any other women seen in Ryan's Bar.
There is also the seedy side of people who spend time drinking with one another in the city without feeling any sense of
loyalty or affection towards one another. Mulvey displays dis-
dain for everyone, particularly his wife and Halloran, a shady
character whose suitcase they are holding as a type of guar-

antee of payment for work they have carried out for him.[6] Their aimless wait is reminiscent of Beckett's characters in *Waiting for Godot*. At times, their conversations have an absurd flavour also. Take, for example, the reaction of Kelly, a man whose sharp comments are a feature of the drinking circle, to Claire Mulvey telling the narrator she's glad he's there. Kelly interjects: "Is he?" "Is he what?", Mulvey asked. "Is he here? Am I here?" (*CS*, 229). This is clearly Beckettian in tone. The characters' wait is punctuated by serious drinking and some stories, most of which are interrupted.

The Mulveys' daughter is neglected by her parents and their house is cold and bare — there is hardly any furniture. There is an atmosphere of putrefaction in the story that is linked to the city and to the thistledown that can be seen floating on the air. The narrator sees the first thistledown as they await Halloran's arrival in the pub: "its thin, pale parachute drifting so slowly across the open doorway that it seemed to move more in water than in air" (*CS*, 237). Mulvey is able to report that it is the dumps in the city that attract the thistles. Denis Sampson reckons that mention of the "dunghill" is closely linked to Yeats's "foul rag and bone shop of the heart". He also notes that the description by the narrator of how his former girlfriend and he danced under the open sky — the concluding image of the story — is Yeatsian in origin as well:

> The final image seems to allude directly to "the dancer and the dance", the triumphant instance in modernism when the "questioning" is subsumed in a knowledge grounded on the untranslatable image. (Sampson, 1993: 213–14)

There is certainly a change in mood as the narrator recalls how liberating it felt to be dancing in the open, as if controlled by

---

[6] Mulvey writes book reviews, but it is not certain what is the exact nature of the work they have done for Halloran.

the music. Prior to that, Mulvey had provided a far harsher image when assessing the current state of Ireland: "Just old boring Ireland strikes again. Even its principal city has one foot in a manure heap" (*CS*, 238). Halloran, whose suitcase has been discovered to contain women's lingerie, is a hapless figure, but his arrival triggers one of the key moments in the story:

> As he came towards the table, a single thistledown appeared, and seemed to hang for a still moment beyond his shoulder in the doorway. A hand reached out, the small fresh hand of a girl or boy, but before it had time to close, the last pale parachute moved on out of sight as if breathed on by the hand's own movement. (*CS*, 238)

That something so beautiful and evasive should be spawned in a dunghill is paradoxical. The experience alleviates the narrator's suffering and allows him to recollect in a tranquil manner the happy moments he lived as he danced with the woman he loved. The ugliness of the city does not impact on him as negatively as it did the previous day. There is a hint that he is on his way to recovering from the failed affair thanks to his heightened perception of beauty in the ordinary material world of which, up until then, he was largely unaware. It is a similar type of experience to that of Elizabeth Reegan (*The Barracks*) as she observes with astonishment the beauty of the frosty landscape after drawing the blinds one morning.

The narrator in "Parachutes" is at pains to depict the material environment, although, unlike Joyce, he does not seem to feel the need to name streets and buildings. On the Sunday morning after the drinking session with the Mulveys, he mechanically follows the crowd heading to Mass but then escapes to a side street: "There were five steps to each house. The stone was granite. Many of the iron railings were painted blue. Across the street was a dishevelled lilac bush. They'd taught us to notice such things when young" (*CS*, 232). In a fit of rage against his upbringing, he states: "I will have to learn the world all over again" (*CS*, 232). Denis Sampson argues that the character's sense of displacement "intensifies his own loss of meaning; the faiths of childhood, of being at home in the phenomenal world and in God's world, have both evaporated" (Sampson, 1993: 208). But this experience of bewilderment precedes the moment of revelation that will occur as he spots the thistledown through the door of the pub. That this moment should coincide with the arrival of Halloran and the boy (a relationship that would cause more furore today than at the time in which the story is set) is indicative of the importance of waiting in the quest for revelation.

Social commentary is prevalent in *The Collected Stories*. The Irish emigrants working in England ("Hearts of Oak and Bellies of Brass", "Faith, Hope and Charity"), the marginalisation of Irish Protestants ("Eddie Mac", "The Conversion of William Kirkwood"), the rituals associated with the land, problems with sexuality, alcohol abuse, these are all touched on in one or several stories. What we have at the end of the book is a rich canvas of vignettes that combine to sketch an outline of human existence as lived out by Irish people at home and abroad. McGahern's canvas complies with the famous observation of Thoreau: "The mass of men live lives of quiet desperation."

Memory Regained

Any mention of the concept of memory regained will inevitably invite a comparison with Proust, one of McGahern's favourite writers. But Proust is only one of many to have explored the concept of how memory can impact in a powerful manner on our perception of time and existence — that said, no one has quite matched his skill in evoking it in his massive work, *A la recherche du temps perdu*.

"The Recruiting Officer" relates a day in the life of a disillusioned school teacher who finds himself back in Arigna: "Now I am growing old in the school where I began" (CS, 100). He is the unenthusiastic witness of a fierce beating of a boy called Walshe by the Manager of the school, Canon Reilly. Walshe is given a choice between a flogging with a length of electric wire and a possible incarceration in the reformatory — understandably, he opts for the former. The priest's "heavy breathing" (CS, 103) indicates both the physical exertion he puts into the punishment and the sexual excitement he derives from administering it. The teacher displays no moral support for Canon Reilly's assertion that an example had to be made of the boy. He is not in favour of such violence but is forced to accept that it is part of the school system. He knows how he is perceived in the area: "It is rumoured that I drink too much" (CS, 100), and that the Canon is not happy about his living above a public house in the nearby town. (The Canon's discontent is related to the fact that he wants the teacher to do religious instruction after second Mass every Sunday which the latter avoids by giving the excuse that it's too far for him to travel.)

Watching the Canon shake a confession out of Walshe — "much as a dog shakes life out of a rat" (CS, 100) — his mind flits back to the time he spent as a trainee Christian Brother. He remembers how they were brought to the sea by the Novicemaster O'Grady: "in threes, less risk of buggery the threes than pairs" (CS, 101) — he clearly held the moral character of the young men in high regard! The routine never changed:

> The bell for night prayers went at nine-thirty, the two rows of pews stretching to the altar, a row along each wall and the bare lino-covered space between empty of all furniture, and we knelt in the long rows in order

of our rank; the higher the rank the closer to the altar. (*CS*, 101)

At a certain stage, he discovered that he didn't have a vocation. However, rather than admit his dilemma to his Superiors, he decided to refuse to leave his bed in the days preceding Final Vows although there was clearly nothing the matter with him. As a result, he was dismissed from the order.

The Canon announces that there will be a visit that afternoon by a Christian Brother who will talk to the boys about possibly devoting their lives to the service of God. The teacher, located outside, can hear the voice drifting through the window:

> If one could only wait long enough everything would be repeated. I wonder who'll rise to the gleaming spoon and find the sharpened hooks as I did once. (*CS*, 108)

He recalls how he was brought home all those years ago by a Brother to discuss things with his parents. He put a compelling case: the child would receive a good education, be respected because of his position. But the greatest motivation of his parents had been the fact that his mother wanted the few acres for his brother. He brings his mother to the sea every year now and she complains bitterly about the brother and his wife. He walks by her side and lets her ramble on, "for it is all a wheel" (*CS*, 110).

The teacher is disillusioned with his work and finds himself watching the clock, willing it around to the hour when he can start cycling towards the town: "I am always happy at this hour. It's as if the chains of the day were worth wearing to feel them drop away" (*CS*, 111). There is no moment of revelation or joy in this character's recollection of times gone by and at the end of the story the "several infusions of whiskey" (*CS*, 111) seem like his only recompense for doing a job that he dislikes. Although his mind wanders back to the past, he is always conscious of what is happening in the present and there is nothing uplifting about his "memory regained".

In "A Slip-up", the old man who stands waiting for his wife to collect him after completing her shopping in Tesco's (London) is living in the past. The daily visits to the super-market remind him of the time he used to accompany his mother as a child when she went shopping. The man and his wife decided to sell their land and move to London. Michael (as the man is called) does not, however, leave his farm be-hind him. Every day, he imagines himself performing different tasks:

> This morning as he walked with Agnes he decided to clear the drinking pool which was dry after the long spell of good weather. First he shovelled the dark earth of rotted leaves and cowshit out on the bank. . . . When he followed the stream to the boundary hedge he found water blocked there. He released it and then leaned on his shovel in the simple pleasure of watching the water flow. (CS, 129–30)

Every now and again he wonders where Agnes can be. He is totally absorbed in his imaginary work on the farm and thinks that she will call him soon for tea. What he doesn't realise is that she has forgotten to collect him after finishing her shop-ping. When she does finally locate him, he is disorientated and confused. He doesn't really want to go to the pub that evening as he is aware that the landlord, Denis, who had driven his wife back to Tesco's to collect him, knows about his "slip-up". James Whyte argues that Michael is becoming increasingly detached from the real world and returning more and more to a child's world, free of responsibility: "He is moving closer and closer towards death, which we know will come when the entire farm has been reclaimed and Michael has completely abandoned the real, unsatisfactory, foreign, urban world" (Whyte, 2002: 195). As we grow old, there is a tendency to return to the world of childhood which assumes a vividness and a reality that are sometimes absent in the present. I agree with Whyte that Michael's death is imminent and I would add that this proximity throws his conception of time into disarray.

"The Wine Breath" illustrates how the barriers of time and place can fall away and enable a person to experience "memory regained", a process that overturns our normal understanding of chronological time. The priest-protagonist is the beneficiary of a heightened awareness of the circular path of his life, of the wheel that allows him to relive the past in the present. The process is triggered by his visit to a parishioner, Gillespie, who is sawing. The way the sun reflects on the sawdust transports him back to the occasion of the burial of Michael Bruen thirty years previously. The day of the funeral, it had been difficult to carry the coffin to the cemetery on Killeelan Hill (which is also mentioned in "A Country Funeral") because of a heavy fall of snow the previous night. The funeral had left an indelible mark on his consciousness: "Never before or since had he experienced the Mystery in such awesomeness" (CS, 179). Now, however, he does not feel awe or terror, just the vividness of the images of a lost day: "He did not know how long he had stood in that lost day, in that white light, probably for no more than a moment. He could not have stood the intensity for any longer" (CS, 179).

When he returns to the present, he sees his hand still on the bar of Gillespie's gate and he feels a little "vulnerable" (CS, 179) because of the vividness of what he has experienced: "Everything in that remembered day was so pure and perfect that he felt purged of all tiredness, was, for a moment, eager to begin life again" (CS, 180). Once more we are dealing with a man who, on the threshold of death, relives events in his life, particularly those of his childhood: "Ever since his mother's death he found himself stumbling into these dead days. Once, crushed mint in the garden had given him back a day he'd spent with her at the sea with such reality that he had been frightened, as if he'd suddenly fallen through time; it was as if the world of the dead was as available to him as the world of the living" (*CS*, 180). Denis Sampson draws a comparison between this "falling through time" and Gabriel Conroy's situation at the end of "The Dead" (Sampson, 1993: 175). The similarities relate to the spiritual nature of the experience of the two men. The priest realises the importance of the day he is living: "the day from which our salvation had to be won or lost" but "with nothing of the eternal other than it would dully endure" (*CS*, 180). He contrasts this with the "day set alight in his mind by the light of the white beech, though it had been nothing more than a funeral he had attended during a dramatic snowfall when a boy, seemed bathed in the eternal, seemed everything we had been taught and told of the world of God" (*CS*, 180).

This "epiphany" renders him dissatisfied when he awakes from his reverie and he decides to avoid meeting the Gillespies in order to be able to immerse himself once more in his memories. He recalls the evening he visited Michael Bruen's house, the sumptuous meal that was handed up to him. He then recalls the time he spent with his mother before her death when she had slipped into senility. He senses that his own death is not too far away and that his memories are a means of escaping the stark reality of his mortality: "it was out of fear of death he became a priest, which became in time the fear of life" (*CS*, 183). Through a succession of insights, he is able to view his life objectively and to see the futility of hiding from the growing shadow of eternity:

> Then, quietly, he saw that he had a ghost all right, one that he had been walking around with for a long time, a ghost he had not wanted to recognize — his own death. He might as well get to know him well. (*CS*, 187)

This is close to the experience of Gabriel Conroy in "The Dead" who notes: "One by one, they were all becoming shades. Better pass boldly into that other world, in the full glory of some passion, than fade and wither dismally with age" (Joyce, 1996: 255). By accepting the reality of their death, the priest and Gabriel Conroy come to understand more fully God, the Other, the vastness of eternity. There can be no doubt that the process of "regaining" memory brings the priest closer to God as he feels "himself immersed in time without end" (CS, 187). In undertaking this journey back in time he recreates for us a world and a life that no longer exist outside of memory. This is the type of literary goal McGahern gives himself also, that of recreating through style a vision of existence with which his readers can commune. *The Collected Stories* provide us with snapshots of existence, sketches of intense moments in the lives of ordinary human beings raised to the stature of universal figures who are readily identifiable as real people.

When summing up the significance of Joyce's *Dubliners*, McGahern was prompted to write: "I do not see *Dubliners* as a book of separate stories. The whole work has more the unity and completeness of a novel" (McGahern, 1991a: 36). The same claim could be made about *The Collected Stories*. The "vivid sections of the wheel", evoked in the opening story, do eventually manage to capture the evasive grail, the "rich whole", in the pursuit of which the author is constantly engaged. His two most recently published novels, which are the subject of the final chapter, confirm my thesis that the quest has yielded a rich harvest.

Chapter Four

Swansong of Rural Ireland: *Amongst Women* and *That They May Face the Rising Sun*

Amongst Women

The positive responses elicited by McGahern's two most recent novels have been almost universal. Even critics like John Cronin, who had difficulty with some of the earlier works, declared that *Amongst Women* "achieves a powerful unity of effect" and that it "is a stylistically seamless work" (Cronin, 1992: 169, 173). Cronin reckons that it manages this because it reverts to what McGahern described as the "inner formality or calm" in the Preface to the second edition of *The Leavetaking* and he adds:

> With a blessedly saving self-awareness, McGahern has, in *Amongst Women*, moved away from what he identified as the "crudity" of the second part of *The Leavetaking*, a crudity repeated in *The Pornographer*, and has reverted to the controlled, observant mode which has served him so well in his first novel, *The Barracks*. The stylistic success . . . seems all the more

impressive when one considers how entirely familiar much of the detail is. (Cronin, 1992: 174)

The discussion of the previous works has highlighted McGahern's struggle to find a voice that would suit his material. *The Barracks* was a promising start but in the novels that followed we see a tendency to experiment with style and with the novel form, a tendency that did not always enjoy the most felicitous results. But throughout his literary career, McGahern has been attempting to find the right way of conveying the image that is at the heart of his creativity. This task brings him on a circular path back to his rural roots in the north-west midlands of Ireland. He returned there at the end of *The Pornographer* and has not left it since. His attitude to this setting has changed considerably. Gone are the pain and the failed struggle to achieve autonomy that characterise young Mahoney's itinerary in *The Dark*. By the time he came to compose *Amongst Women*, McGahern was more at ease with his medium and with himself. This could explain why Fintan O'Toole found the novel "completely Irish and highly universal" (O'Toole, 1990). Through the use of the image, he sets about transforming the world, a process which is not without its pitfalls:

> Image after image flows involuntarily now, and still we are not at peace, rejecting, altering, shaping, straining towards the one image that will never come, the lost image that gave our lives expression, the image that would completely express it again in this bewilderment between our beginning and end. (McGahern, 1991d: 12)

McGahern's article, "The Image", does not state anything startlingly new about the creative process. It points out how the writer's struggle for "the absurd crown of style", which is the "revelation" in language of our private world, is similar to, and different from, formal religion. McGahern is pessimistic about language's efficacy in capturing some of the more intense moments that take hold of a person in the course of a lifetime. His pessimism is shown to be ill-founded in novels such as *The Barracks*, which provides a telling description of the hopes and fears of a middle-aged woman as she approaches death. It is the books themselves that speak most eloquently of McGahern's achievements as a writer and not any theorising in which he engages about his aesthetic approach.

What ensures that his work will be explored and read for many years to come is his ability to write the swansong of a disappearing civilisation, of the rural Ireland in which he grew up, where he now lives and which provides the backdrop to his best fiction. Many critics have linked *Amongst Women* to Tomás Ó Criomhthain's *An tOileánach*, mainly because of their portrayal of two epical figures fighting against the imminent demise of their race, and certainly there are similarities to be found here. However, I feel Ó Criomhthain's account is much closer in tone and style to *That They May Face the Rising Sun*. I see more similarities between *Amongst Women* and Ernie O'Malley's account of the War of Independence, *On Another Man's Wound*. I will refer briefly to these two works in the course of this chapter, because of their similarities with McGahern's chronicling of a disappearing civilisation. Eamonn Wall maintains:

> *Amongst Women* is a mirror to the century — from the War of Independence to close to the present. Here is a work which functions both as a chronicle of the fortunes of the Moran family and also a chronicle of the fortunes of the nation in its progress through fifty years of change. (Wall, 1999: 305)

James Whyte highlights the polarisation of approach among literary critics who tend to regard McGahern's fiction either in the context of social realism or from an aesthetic perspective. Whyte underlines that neither approach is adequate. Because of the lack of a structured society, a prerequisite for the novel form in the past, McGahern is faced with an amorphousness that causes him to adopt a somewhat different approach: "McGahern is more a romantic idealist than an objective commentator, using his licence as a writer of imaginative fiction to spin history into myth" (Whyte, 2002: 218). Despite the validity of Whyte's doubts with regard to McGahern being a social commentator, he does nevertheless manage to encapsulate many of the changes that took hold of Irish society in the last fifty years, as Wall maintains in the quote above. Once more he manages to do this by concentrating on a single family, living in a detached manner on a farm in the north-west midlands of Ireland. All the elements of change touch the claustrophobic and inward-looking Great Meadow, the name given to the farm inhabited by the Moran family.

Michael Moran displays qualities associated with several male characters encountered in other works by McGahern: Reegan in *The Barracks*, another disillusioned veteran of the War of Independence, Mahoney senior in *The Dark*, who struggles with the land and finds that he has no one to whom he can bequeath it. There is equally the father in the short story "Gold Watch", whose wife is also called Rose, and others too numerous to mention. In fact, as is pointed out by Antoinette Quinn, "Michael Moran, the peremptory husband and *paterfamilias* of *Amongst Women*, had appeared under a different alias in all the novels, except *The Pornographer*" (Quinn, 1991: 79). Moran is a man whom many readers would find familiar. He is the possessive and domineering husband and father, the centre of attention in Great Meadow, the battleground of his post-guerrilla military campaign. He is not happy with what the fight for Irish freedom has delivered:

> Some of our own johnnies in the top jobs instead of a
> few Englishmen. More than half of my own family
> work in England. What was it all for? The whole thing
> was a cod. (AW, 5)

Because of disgruntlement about the upshot of his "revolution", Moran determines to set up a "Republic" of his own:
the family. After an argument with McQuaid, who was his old-
est and best friend, the one comrade-in-arms with whom he
has maintained contact, Moran begins to see that his influence
is waning on all "fronts". His family are growing up and he realises that he may soon be left on his own. We are told that it
is this prospect that leads to his decision to marry Rose — a
carefully considered "strategy". She will be his accomplice in
ensuring that he remains the centre of attention. When he
thinks about the loss of McQuaid's friendship, he is consoled
by the thought of a ready-made replacement: "families were
what mattered, more particularly that larger version of himself
— *his* family; and while seated in the same scheming fury he
saw each individual member gradually slipping out of his reach.
Yes, they would eventually all go" (AW, 22). What he fails to
grasp is that his influence is such on his three daughters and
his younger son, Michael, that they will never really leave him
or Great Meadow, even though they go to live and work
elsewhere. He is the centre of their universe, the one who
gives them an innate sense of their own importance:

> On the tides of Dublin or London they [his daughters]
> were hardly more than specks of froth but together
> they were the aristocratic Morans of Great Meadow, a
> completed world, Moran's daughters. (AW, 2)

This is one of the reasons why the girls attempt to revive
Monaghan Day at the beginning of the novel — Monaghan
Day was the name given to the end-of-February fair in Mohill
that was also the occasion when McQuaid made his annual
visit to the house. (It is also referred to in *That They May Face
the Rising Sun.*) Unaware of the argument between the two
men that put an end to the visits, the daughters feel that it
might revive their father a bit if he were to have an opportunity to talk about the War and his old friend, now deceased.

The tension that they endured on these occasions in the past is forgotten. With distance, Monaghan Day "had become large, heroic, blood-mystical, something from which the impossible could be snatched" (AW, 2).[1] Although resentful of any effort to dredge up the past, Moran is obliged to recount some of his experiences of the War. He refuses to romanticise what he was part of. He tells them: "It was a bad business." He and his comrades were "a bunch of killers" (AW, 5).

He does go on to make one very important point, however, concerning the intensity of the experiences he and his comrades lived through during that time:

> For people like McQuaid and myself the war was the best part of our lives. Things were never so simple and clear again. I think we never rightly got the hang of it afterwards. It was better if it had never happened. (AW, 6)

This invites a comparison with O'Malley's classic account of life in the Flying Columns, *On Another Man's Wound*. O'Malley's peregrinations around the Irish countryside gave him the uplifting conviction that he was helping to make history: "I lived on a mountain top where there was no need for speech, even. I felt an understanding, a sharing of something bigger than ourselves, and a heightening of life" (O'Malley, 1979: 61). This sentiment echoes that of Moran very closely: there is a feeling that life never regains the intensity of the war-time experience. Both O'Malley and Moran are struggling for a cause that they hold dear and yet they are torn between their ideals and a sometimes indifferent or hostile public.

Declan Kiberd notes that O'Malley has a wonderful capacity for capturing the rural landscape, particularly at night as he is moving through it: "Seeing the lights flashing in the windows

---

[1] The vocabulary used, so close to Padraig Pearse's description of the 1916 Rising, is too obvious not to have been deliberate.

of country kitchens. And seeing, on the one hand, a tenderness towards the people but also a tremendous sense of estrangement from them. He cannot afford to mingle with these people in whose name, nevertheless, he is fighting to free a country, and to reshape the meaning of Ireland" (Maher and Kiberd, 2002: 88–9). Kiberd goes on to say that there is the touch of the artist about this predicament in that the artist is similarly bound up with the people but, because of his attempts to represent them, forever estranged from them also. McGahern has written about O'Malley in a way that shows he appreciates in a particular way the style the latter uses to describe his experiences in *On Another Man's Wound*. In a review of a new edition of the book in 1996, McGahern displays a clear affinity with the objective being pursued by O'Malley:

> When young, he had absorbed a myth and was prepared to follow it, like a single flame, no matter what the cost was to himself or to others. . . . The work has imaginative truth. What is so extraordinary is not the material itself but that most of it is so well written. (McGahern, 1996a)

Again we see the emphasis he places on style. His admiration for Ó Criomhthain's *An tOileánach* is largely a result of its sculpted style, which he describes as "a persistent way of seeing" (McGahern, 1987: 7). He is not impressed by affectation or prettification.[2] He likes a style that reflects the character

---

[2] In an excellent article tracing the links between McGahern and Proust, Denis Sampson quotes the French writer's comments on style and says that McGahern paraphrased the following quote from Proust in the opening paragraph of "The Image": "Style is not at all a prettification as certain people think. It is not even a matter of technique, it is — like colour with painters — a quality of vision, the revelation of the private universe that each one of us can see and which others cannot see" (Sampson, 1991: 57).

of the writer, the depth of feeling that it conveys.[3] O'Malley, like McGahern, has an affinity with the Irish landscape and the following passage could quite conceivably have been written by the novelist:

> Trees thrusting upwards with added power or bulking sideways; they were arrogant at night, they filled the mind and they ruled the dark. Trees, shrubs, bushes and woods took possession and through them old nature showed its untamed strength and freshness and made us see how small we were, stars helped them to widen the external world. Familiar landscapes changed, hills played tricks in the moonlight and roads became mysterious. (O'Malley, 1979: 138)

There is a close identification with the land, the trees, all of nature in O'Malley's writing that echoes what we find in many passages in McGahern — it also contains a poetic quality that is evident in the lines just quoted.

It is important to understand the impact of the war on some of the characters of *Amongst Women*. Moran's struggle begins, in a sense, after the war has ended. He buys a farm with his army gratuity and begins his attempt to bring order and control to bear on both the land and his family. In his frenetic efforts to eke out a living, however, he doesn't "see" the land that he is farming, cannot appreciate its beauty. The end of the novel shows him going out regularly to the meadow at the back of the house, a fact that causes Mona to say to Rose: "He must see something there" (*AW*, 179). For some reason, this causes both women to burst out crying. Without meaning to, Mona has sensed that her father's pre-

---

[3] In his essay on Ó Criomhthain's *An tOileánach*, he states: "If we think of style as the man, of style as the revelation of personality in language and that the quality of the personality is more important than the material out of which the pattern is shaped." (McGahern, 1987: 7)

occupation with the meadow is linked in some way to his imminent death. Moran, on the threshold of dying, "sees" the splendour that surrounds him for the first time:

> To die was never to look on all this again. It would live in others' eyes but not in his. He had never realized when he was in the midst of confident life what an amazing glory he was part of. (*AW*, 179).

Observations such as these give the reader an idea of what makes *Amongst Women* such a special novel. We perceive the world through Moran's eyes towards the end of his life and we become conscious that he is expressing a universal truth. After a serious illness, daily routine and ordinary scenes assume a charm and a vividness that they never possessed before. Similarly, when death is imminent, the material world takes on a glory that is linked to the thought of never being able to behold it again. (Elizabeth Reegan in *The Barracks* had the same insight.)

For most of the novel, we don't get many insights into what Moran is feeling. He is mainly seen through the eyes of his wife and children. He doesn't say much, but his comments rarely surprise because they are so consistent with the picture that has been drawn of his character. We are conscious that he is irascible and intolerant, domineering and violent, but towards the end of the novel, especially when he stumbles blindly into the meadow, we have a real sense of his vulnerability. He is a man who has been moulded by his environment and by the time he spent as a guerrilla fighter. As is pointed out by Denis Sampson: "Moran's inability to love is clearly linked to his training in hatred, to his skill as an assassin" (Sampson, 1993: 228). There are times, nevertheless, when he arouses anger because of his self-absorption and his miserliness. This is brought to light by his petulance in making it all but impossible for Sheila to study medicine, mainly because of his belief that the medical profession and the priests profited to a greater extent than any other class from Independence. There is also his fear that seven years of medical studies, even with a scholarship, would cost him money. His claim that all his children are equal in his eyes is just an excuse not to allow his daughter follow her dream. It also displays a traditional mindset that had trouble understanding how a woman could become a doctor.

He is capable of vicious verbal assaults such as the one he launches against Rose who, unaware of the full extent of the rift that exists between her husband and his elder son, describes Luke's telegram saying he'll meet Maggie off the train in London as "polite enough" (AW, 52). Stung by her reaction, Moran bides his time but eventually gains his revenge by asking: "Did you ever listen carefully to yourself, Rose? . . . If you listened a bit more carefully to yourself I think you might talk a lot less" (AW, 54). If that wasn't bad enough, his second "shot" (his prowess with the rifle is often commented on) some time later when she is trying to redecorate the house (with her own money, an independence that Moran does not appreciate) strikes straight to her heart: "There's no need for you to be turning the whole place upside down. We managed well enough before you ever came round the place" (AW, 69).

On this second occasion, Rose threatens to leave Great Meadow, a threat that frightens Moran because of how he lost his son Luke following an argument and a particularly severe beating he administered to him. He has to apologise to the woman whom he is shocked to discover he knows even less well now than before they were married. He had driven her to the point where she "could give up no more ground and live" (AW, 71). This is a wonderfully evocative expression, linking the land issue to the emotional landscape — a very important link in this novel.

After their first argument, there is a wonderful moment when they make up but don't kiss, although alone. We are told: "That belonged to darkness and the night" (AW, 56). This captures the type of sexual propriety that existed in Ireland a number of decades ago. Sexuality is dealt with in a discreet and circumspect manner in *Amongst Women* — there is no attempt to shock or disturb. Moran's courtship of Rose is classical in its tact. The meetings in the post office develop into an invitation to Rose's house, a return visit from her to meet his "troops". Her mother is not at all keen on the match but is not prepared to be discourteous to a visitor: "Though her mother disliked him the custom of hospitality was too strict to allow any self-expression or unpleasantness" (*AW*, 28–9). John Cronin says that "this rustic wooing is delicately and entertainingly observed" (Cronin, 1992: 173). He also comments on how young Michael on the morning of his father's wedding draws "free from the kneading hand" (*AW*, 39), and adds: "One notes the authorial tact which makes this revealing passage so very different from the incestuous abuse of young Mahoney by his father in *The Dark*" (Cronin, 1992: 175). While I agree with Cronin's appreciation of the portrayal of the courtship, I don't accept that the depiction of Moran with his son is in any way similar to that of Mahoney's abuse. There is "authorial tact" in *Amongst Women* but it doesn't apply to the scene to which Cronin refers. We are meant to feel uncomfortable at the abuse of young Mahoney in *The Dark* — there is no other way to convey the horror of such abuse — whereas nothing untoward is suspected in *Amongst Women*. Moran isn't the sort of man who would stoop so low as to abuse his children sexually, even though he has no compunction about subjecting them to emotional blackmail, another form of abuse. He is a different type of man altogether to Mahoney: he is more honourable and secure in his cult of family.

There is clearly "authorial tact" evident in the description of the wedding night of Rose and Moran, however. The children imagine with some discomfort what is happening in the marital bedroom:

> They tried not to breathe as they listened. They were
> too nervous and frightened of life to react to or to
> put into words the sounds they heard from the room
> where their father was sleeping with Rose. (*AW*, 48)

Controlled prose, consistent characterisation, these are the distinguishing features of *Amongst Women*. The book tells of arrivals and departures, all of which are remarkably similar: children growing to independence, getting married, having children of their own, the reciting of the rosary, making hay, going to the train station to collect people and drop them off. The narrative has a timeless, universal quality. There is not a lot by way of plot: the book is held together by its style and its wonderful sketching of how the different characters relate to Moran and their home, Great Meadow. Moran is someone we love and hate, but cannot ignore. There are no chapter divisions in the novel and it is clear that everything has been honed to its bare essentials. Antoinette Quinn says it is "a spare, scaled down novel, concentrating on one family and farmhouse in a remote Irish village" (Quinn, 1991: 79). John Banville, reviewing the novel in *The Observer* (7 May 1990), notes: "We have the feeling that we have not so much been reading as living." This is a significant assessment coming from a novelist such as Banville, who is not noted for the sort of traditional realism which characterises *Amongst Women*. Even more insightful in my opinion is the assessment of Fintan O'Toole:

> What strikes you most forcefully about it is its apparent simplicity, its uniformity of tone, the way it achieves a single rhythm all the way through, the way it seems to unfold, not over the decades that the story takes, but over a single day, returning as a ballad does, to the first verse at the end. This seems simple until you think: "Who else has managed to do this, to create a big, powerful novel that still stays within a single frame, in modern Ireland?" (O'Toole, 1990)

O'Toole recognises that McGahern's originality lies in his refusal to conform to fashion. He also sees that the novel manages to record the story of modern Ireland faithfully and convincingly. He refers to McGahern's essay on *An tOileánach* and especially to his comment about Ó Criomhthain's account where "people and place seem to stand outside history". That prompts O'Toole to state:

> And this is precisely what *Amongst Women* deals with. You start off thinking that it is about Irish history, about a man who fought in the War of Independence and what happens to him afterwards. But you realise as you go on that it is about the *absence* of history, about the country that was *not* formed, the community that did *not* come into existence, the society that did *not* grow. (O'Toole, 1990)

McGahern is a social realist with a romantic bent. He relates to Moran's disappointment of the Ireland that *failed* to emerge and his attempts to transcend the social reality that surrounds him by creating the independent republic of Great Meadow.

All this is conveyed in a delicate and tactful manner: the form reflects the content. Declan Kiberd says: "I think John always recognised that style was the challenge. And the style must never be self-conscious" (Maher and Kiberd, 2002: 90). In discussing the similarity between McGahern and Flaubert, he mentions the latter's comment about when a good writer describes a flower, the reader doesn't think: what fine writing. Rather, he should think what a fine thing a flower is. This goes to the core of what gives McGahern his cutting edge. Each reader gets something different from *Amongst Women*:

> I would say that *Amongst Women* is one of the major books of the last fifty years in Ireland. And it may, in fact, be the book that most fully gathers together the feeling of what it was like to live through that process in Ireland. (Maher and Kiberd, 2002: 91)

As distinct from the Big House novel, this is a "Small House" novel, depicting the last moments of a rural-based, family-centred unit, held together by certain religious principles and a (diminished) belief in the pillars of Irish society: the Church and State. Great Meadow and its inhabitants are as separate from the surrounding landscape as any Big House ever was.

There is a significant passage describing how the family, after the departure of Mona and Sheila to work in Dublin, kneel down to say the rosary. For the first time, the vulnerability of the house becomes clear:

> A wind was swirling round the house, sometimes gusting in the chimney, and there was an increasing sense of fear as the trees stirred in the storm outside when the prayers ended. For the first time the house seemed a frail defence against all that beat around it. (AW, 90)

One can sense Moran's frustration on coming to the realisation that it is virtually impossible to protect his family from outside influences. The winds of change were blowing around Great Meadow in the same way as they were taking hold of the rest of Ireland.

The motor car is a symbol of this change. While Moran only uses it for special occasions like going to the train station or visiting Rose's family, the returned emigrant, Nell Morahan, who has made money in the US, uses hers for transporting Michael (her fifteen-year-old lover) and herself around the country. One trip they make to Strandhill bears a strong resemblance to the journey made by Moran and Rose after the first argument concerning Luke. Anne Goarzin (2002: 63–72) provides an interesting analysis of the similarities and differences in both accounts. Moran attempts to make it up to Rose for their contretemps by bringing her off for the day. He replies to her question about where they can go by saying: "We can drive anywhere we want to. That's the great thing about having a car. All we have to do is back it out of the shed and go" (*AW*, 56). The irony contained in this comment about the freedom having a car affords a couple, is not lost on the reader when Nell and young Michael begin their affair, an affair that is rendered more feasible by the fact that Nell possesses a car. Both couples park near the old cannon, go for a walk on the beach (the older couple are satisfied with pointing out Rosses Point in the distance, whereas the younger couple go all the way up to it) and there is a series of descriptions that brings into focus the irony that is cleverly deployed to highlight the different behaviour and customs of the two couples. After eating tea and sandwiches prepared by Rose, Moran declares: "I feel like a new man" (*AW*, 59). His hunger is mirrored by young Michael's sexual appetite as he and Nell make love in the dunes:

> When he entered her for the third time she was ready to search for her own pleasure and he was now able to wait. Such was her strength that he was frightened. She shouted, seized him roughly at the hips and forced him to move; and when it was over she opened her eyes and with her hands held his face for a quick, grateful kiss he couldn't comprehend. (*AW*, 105)

Michael, like his father, feels like "a new man" after making love. The "grateful kiss" given to him by Nell is echoed by Moran's recital of the Grace after meals: "We give thee thanks, O Almighty God, for all Thy bounty we have received" (*AW*, 59). These parallels are not accidental. And so we have the slight difference in the order in which the two couples carry out the different activities of walking and eating (a symbolic meal of the flesh in the case of the younger couple), observing the ocean, picking shellfish in the pools of water, seeing people on the beach, parking the car. These differences underline the fact that much has changed in the way the generations behave.

When Moran talks about the holidays the family spent in Strandhill, he proudly recounts how they sold turf as a way of paying for the holiday. Michael is embarrassed when he recalls how his father made them go from house to house:

> "It was horrible going round the houses," he betrayed the same sense of separateness the father had instilled in the others, which was plainly less than useful when it came to selling turf. "You'd feel like crawling into a hole." (AW, 106)

Such authorial commentary is not usual in this novel: it is plainly the desire of the narrator to point out how the father and son have a completely different worldview that is in keeping with the pace of social change. Michael lives through the sexual revolution that began to take hold of Ireland during the 1960s — it was prevalent in Dublin before it spread to the countryside. The anonymous narrator of *The Pornographer* provides a picture of the capital with its young inhabitants shedding the inhibitions of their parents and the control of the Church in order to indulge their sexual urges. Michael's affair with Nell shows him to be a far different man from his father. (One suspects that Moran senior's character wouldn't have been so dissimilar to his father's.) Michael doesn't display any sign of guilt about what he is doing. If anything, his affair and the lovemaking energise him and make him long for independence. Such a desire sets him on a collision course with his father.

Back from his day at the beach with Nell (where his burgeoning manhood had been affirmed), he is forced to assume once more a subservient role and help his father with the sheep. When the job is finished, Moran turns to express his gratitude only to find that his son has gone. He dwells poignantly on what could be achieved if the two of them were to run the farm:

> He had forgotten how good two people could be working together. A man working alone was nothing. If the boy wanted to come in with him the two of them could do anything. They could run this place like clockwork. They could in time even take over other farms, a dream he had once had about his eldest son: together they could take over everything. (*AW*, 108)

This is just another example of an unfulfilled Moran dream and it makes the reader more sympathetic to his plight. His sons don't possess their father's attachment to the land and they end up living in London, a city that is about as stark a contrast as you'd find with Great Meadow. In Michael's case, however, the rift with Moran is not definitive.

The great regret that Moran carries with him to the grave is his inability to bring about a reconciliation with Luke. The daughters tend to romanticise their memories of home, blotting out the bad moments: "In London or Dublin the girls would look back to the house for healing. The remembered light on the empty hayfields would grow magical . . . when they were away the house would become the summer light and shade above their whole lives" (*AW*, 85). Luke, on the other hand, has a sharper sense of what really went on. When Maggie and her husband Mark try to persuade him to visit his father, saying that he holds too much of a grudge, Luke responds: "I hold no grudge. That would be stupid. But I have a good memory" (*AW*, 143).

McQuaid's break with Moran is largely due to his refusal to continue playing a subordinate role (he had been Moran's junior officer during the war) and his last words spell that out clearly as he climbs into his Mercedes: "Some people just cannot bear to come in second" (*AW*, 22). This is an accurate assessment of Moran's predicament. He is a man who wants to live in the past, a glorious past when he was young, brave, alive. He resents the fact that McQuaid has become rich as a cattle dealer while he is forced to work hard in the fields to make a living — in social terms he has definitely come in "second".

The old male desire to be "top dog", reinforced by his military training, is also what alienates him from Luke. McQuaid says: "I always liked Luke. He is very straight and manly" (AW, 13), a comment that infuriates Moran. Luke maintains that "only women can live with Daddy" and then goes on to say:

> "I didn't choose my father. He didn't choose me. If I'd known, I certainly would have refused to meet the man. No doubt he'd have done likewise with me."
> (AW, 144)

Luke is wide of the mark in that assessment of his father. For Moran, the family is sacrosanct. He repeatedly urges his children to always behave in a way that will reflect their uniqueness. It is true that his "cult" of family also suits his own purposes. The daily recitation of the rosary, from which the title of the novel is taken, glorifies the position of the father in the opening prayer of each decade, the *Our Father*, and the closing words, "Glory be to the Father and to the Son and to the Holy Spirit". This patriarchal domination is one that was condoned and implemented by the Catholic Church and the Irish State in the decades after Independence.[4] It was based on blind allegiance and obedience. Moran is portrayed as being no better or worse than other Irish fathers of the time.

---

[4] Rüdiger Imhof offers the following assessment of the novel: "*Amongst Women* . . . analyses the emotional restriction, the narrow sanctimoniousness and the patriarchy that characterised life in Ireland in the 1950s and 1960s. It offers a study of the intimidating and infuriating tensions as well as the appeasing rituals that weld the Moran family together so that the members may largely ignore the passage of time" (Imhof, 2002: 236).

McQuaid treats his wife in an appalling manner, bringing a group of men to the house at unexpected moments and ordering her to get a meal ready. Moran at least imparts a sense of their own importance to his children. As Maggie is heading off to London, he offers her this piece of advice: "You never know how low or high you'll go. No matter how you rise in the world never look down on another. That way you can never go far wrong" (AW, 61). Maggie drinks in his words, which have an added poignancy because of the circumstances in which they are uttered.

Luke is the thorn in his side, the one who has escaped from his sphere of influence. Each time Maggie or Michael come home from London, Moran eagerly seeks information about "that brother of yours". Finally he takes pen to paper in one of the classic moments of the novel and even goes so far as to offer an apology. The style of the letter reflects both the age and the emotion of the person who is writing it:

> Let me say that I had no wish to harm you in the past and I have no wish to harm you in the future and if I have done so in thought, word or deed I am sorry. The daffodils are nearly in bloom, also shrubs, flowers, fruit etc. It'll soon be time for planting. Tired now and of that thought, who cares anyhow? Daddy.

On reading the letter, Luke rightly concludes that his father is growing old. He replies saying that there is nothing to forgive and that he doesn't hold any grudge. At the same time, he does not travel home to visit the dying man. Too much has happened between them for any sort of normal relationship to resume. The references to nature, which is on the verge of rebirth, and the contrast between it and his own tiredness, show how Moran feels his end is near.

It is worth noting that his letter-writing style bears more than a passing resemblance to that of McGahern: "He had a clear, bare style: when writing he seemed to be able to slip

the burden of his personality as he could never face to face"
(*AW*, 66). The repetitious nature of Moran's language, with its
refrains ("Who cares anyhow", "All my children are equal in
my eyes") and cadences, "echoes the rhythms of prayer and
the bible" (Whyte, 2002: 209). It also serves to emphasise the
immutability of Great Meadow in the eyes of the children
who return to it.

Significantly, the novel begins and ends with the women.
The power shifts from Moran to his wife and daughters as he
grows weaker. After his marriage to Rose, we are told how
she and the girls become "conspirators". "They were mastered and yet they were controlling together what they were
mastered by" (*AW*, 46). Later, when they come to the realisation that Moran is about to die, they bring all their combined
strength to bear: "Since they had the power of birth there
was no reason why they couldn't will this life free of death"
(*AW*, 178). This naturally proves to be beyond even their
considerable capabilities. However, after the funeral, we are
told that they gain strength from the love that they shared for
"Daddy" and they come to replace him:

> It was as if their first love and allegiance had been
> pledged uncompromisingly to this one house and man
> and that they knew that he had always been at the
> very centre of all parts of their lives. . . . it was as if
> each of them in their different ways had become
> Daddy. (*AW*, 183)

With *Amongst Women*, McGahern has composed one of
the great novels about family life in Irish literature. As it is
portrayed in this novel, families like the Morans are a fast-
disappearing institution. Denis Sampson rightly emphasises
the universal aspect of McGahern's achievement: "Certainly,
McGahern has written a novel of family that resonates across
cultures" (Sampson, 1993: 231). *That They May Face the Rising
Sun* shows how the family has all but disappeared from the

landscape in the past few decades in parts of rural Ireland. *Amongst Women*, whether that was McGahern's primary purpose or not, is an important chronicle of Irish rural family life. The recent initiative by *The Irish Times* and the James Joyce Centre, A Novel Choice, which invited readers to select the greatest Irish novels in the English language, put *Amongst Women* in third place behind Joyce's *Ulysses* and *A Portrait of the Artist as a Young Man*. Writing in *The Irish Times* (27 September, 2003), Declan Kiberd explained why he rated it as his personal favourite: "It's a signature novel for a generation of Irish people who lived through the last century. It takes the energies and trends of the time and gives them back to the reader in a recognisable form." The spilling of the rosary beads into the hands and the placing of the papers on the floor before the reciting of the prayer, the tensions between conflicting views of authority among children and their parents, tending to the animals, making the hay, nowhere are these rituals better captured than in McGahern's novel.

Some of the high points of *Amongst Women* are the scenes that describe the family working together in the fields. On Maggie's first trip home in the summer from London, Moran cuts the meadow and calls the children into action. They have a strong sense of affinity when they share the labour:

> As they walked away from him through the greenness, the pale blue above them, Maggie said, her voice thick with emotion, "Daddy is just lovely when he's like that". (*AW*, 81)

Mona and Sheila concur. The tension of saving the hay before the rain comes focuses their attention and helps them to forget the pain in their limbs. Moran praises their efforts and at the same time extols the virtues of the family: "Alone we might do nothing. Together we can do anything" (*AW*, 84).

This scene is in sharp contrast to the next time the family gather to save the hay. At this point, both Maggie and Sheila are married and Michael is working in London. Moran has difficulties with the tedder which are sorted out by the local Protestant, Rodden. There is a warmth between Moran and Rodden that might appear not to be in keeping with the former's republican ideals. But the two men share a certain detachment and estrangement from the people around them:

> Though Moran had been a guerrilla fighter from the time he was little more than a boy he had always insisted that his quarrel had never been with Protestants. Now he identified much more with this beleaguered class than his Catholic neighbours. No matter how favourably the tides turned for him he would always contrive to be in permanent opposition. (*AW*, 163)

Sheila's husband, Sean, back from their honeymoon, is out working with them in the fields. His hands blister quickly and Moran observes that he was the son his mother had hoped would become a priest: "He was brought up to be the priesteen" (*AW*, 166). Moran is shrewd in his assessments of his sons-in-law. He can see that Maggie's husband, Mark, is well on the way to becoming a drunkard and that he's all swagger — like some of the men in his column, he'd be no good in a crunch situation. Sheila chooses a man who likes the comforts of middle-class life but who doesn't appreciate the security of a permanent job in the Civil Service, a sentiment that elicits Moran's anger. Both husbands pose no threat to Moran's dominance, however, which explains in part his willingness to accept them into the "family".

When Sean and Sheila retire from the fields to go back to the house, the others continue working in the field. But they are angry at the thought of the couple making love:

> No one spoke in the intense uneasiness, but they
> were forced to follow them in their minds into the
> house, how they must be shedding their clothes, going
> naked towards one another. . . . "You'd think they
> could have waited," Michael said quietly, in agreement
> with the resentment he felt all about him. It was as if
> the couple were together disregarding the inviolability
> of the house, its true virginity, with a selfish absorp-
> tion. (*AW*, 165–6)

There is a double betrayal at work here. Firstly, Sean and
Sheila leave the work in the fields, a labour that has always
been carried out by the whole family and then there's their
making love in the house, disturbing its "true virginity".

Michael, of all people, is not unversed in the ways of the
world but he is the one who speaks for everyone in denounc-
ing the couple for their lack of discretion. He is the last to
leave the meadow with his father, who says: "God bless you
son. That was a great day" (*AW*, 167). As they make their way
back to Great Meadow, there is a lovely evocation of the
happy tiredness of men who have shared hours of labour in
the fields: "Out on the road passing cars had their headlights
on. Across the road, somewhere in the demesne, a single pi-
geon was still cooing its hoarse throaty call as they dragged
their feet through the orchard to the lighted house" (*AW*,
167). Atmospheric descriptions like this one will become
more commonplace in *That They May Face the Rising Sun*, a
novel to which we will turn our attention shortly.

Before leaving *Amongst Women*, I should point out how it
established McGahern as a significant writer. The nomination
for the Booker Prize, even if the writer himself doesn't pay
much attention to prizes, was a sign that the literary Estab-
lishment was being forced to take him seriously. *Amongst
Women* embodies a total world, seen through the lens of a
single family. The characters are presented in their full outline
and with the sort of tact and discretion that would have been

necessary for them to live with one another. His intimate knowledge of the landscape and its people enables McGahern to produce a novel that transcends time and place.

One of the key passages in the book is the paragraph that describes Moran's insight as he walks the land as the light is beginning to fail:

> It was like grasping water to think how quickly the years had passed here. They were nearly gone. It was in the nature of things and yet it brought a sense of betrayal and anger, of never having understood anything much. Instead of using the fields, he sometimes felt as if the fields had used him. Soon they would be using someone else in his place. It was unlikely to be either of his sons. (*AW*, 130)

McGahern said at a reading in Saint Patrick's College, Drumcondra (9 April 2003) that it was when he had written these lines he felt that the novel was going to work. This epiphany, to be experienced again shortly before his death, reveals things that had long remained a mystery to Moran. Everything assumes a cold clarity — the brevity of life, the futility of his blind labour: "He continued walking the fields like a man trying to see" (*AW*, 130). When asked to comment on Moran's reaction to seeing "the amazing glory he was part of" before he dies, Declan Kiberd provides an assessment of the novel that leads in well to our discussion of *That They May Face the Rising Sun*:

> What I think McGahern does in some ways is to return the word [*epiphany*] to the religious context. So a character like Moran has that wonderful vision of the creativity of the world all around him in the bloom of nature in the fields. Although he is a sick man — because he is a sick man — in some way he is restored by this feeling that things will go on. A tradition will live in the lament for its passing . . . And that is where you see McGahern lamenting, making the

swansong, lamenting the decline of some code. He is shrewdly aware that the story he is producing will be part of the next culture. It isn't merely a howl of lament. It's also a piece of procreation. And I think this is the feeling that Moran has at that moment in the book. (Maher and Kiberd, 2002: 96)

That They May Face The Rising Sun

McGahern's latest novel, which appeared almost twelve years after *Amongst Women*, has been hailed as a classic by critics on both sides of the pond. It has been a major commercial success in the US, the first of McGahern's novels to have made such an impact over there, where its title was changed to *By the Lake*. Some readers (a minority, I hasten to add), loyal to McGahern down the years, have not been so impressed, however. They are somewhat bemused at the lack of plot or of character development. Their unease can be explained to some extent by the fact that it is not a novel in the conventional sense, more a lyrical evocation of a particular place and its inhabitants. There comes a stage in a writer's career where he or she is acknowledged as being capable of producing "great literature" — this is now the case with McGahern. Only William Trevor among contemporary Irish writers enjoys a similar stature: John Banville, Colm Toibín, Roddy Doyle, Jennifer Johnston are close to achieving it also.

Having said all that, *That They May Face the Rising Sun* is a wonderful book and is a fitting conclusion to McGahern's swansong to Irish rural life. Writing in *The Guardian* (12 January 2002), Seamus Deane notes how the novel has a serenity and a gentleness that were not in evidence in much of McGahern's earlier fiction:

This book is a strange and wonderful mixture of various genres of writing — narrative in the basic sense, but also a meditation, a memoir, a retrospect, an

anthropological study of a community, . . . a celebration of an Ireland that had formerly been the object of
chill analysis as well as loving evocation. All these aspects are contained within a capacious style that has
all the lucidity and intensity we have become accustomed to in McGahern, but inflected by a tone of for-
giveness and acceptance that adds an amplitude and
serenity rarely achieved in fiction.

Deane is correct in mentioning the mixture of the various
genres that McGahern uses in this novel to produce what is
in essence "an anthropological study of a community" — I
would add, "that is on the verge of extinction". Nobody in
this community is under the age of fifty and there doesn't
seem to be much hope that their like will be found again —
this is where the link with Ó Criomhthain's pronouncement
at the end of An tOileánach comes in: Ní bheidh ár leithéidí arís
ann (our like will not be there again).[5] Declan Kiberd says
that An tOileánach is a little like "an anthropological textbook"
(Kiberd, 2000: 526) and he has made parallels between
McGahern's literary project and that of Ó Criomhthain in
their depiction of how cultures and civilisations that are in
terminal decline attain a lyrical and elegiac utterance before
they lie down and die. Patrick Ryan, the rough-tongued but
loyal handyman, recognises at the end of the novel that things
are coming to an end when he says to Ruttledge:

> "We're going to finish that building. . . . It takes a hard
> jolt every now and again to learn us that we'll not be
> in it for ever." (RS, 297)

---

[5] I think the full quote is necessary in order to show the way in which the
objective of the account is spelled out: "I have written minutely of much
that we did, for it was my wish that somewhere there should be a memorial of it all, and I have done my best to set down the character of the people about me so that some record of us might live after us, for the like of
us will never be again." (Ó Criomhthain, 2000: 244.)

Even more tellingly, he says:

> "After us there'll be nothing but the water hen and
> the swan." (*RS*, 45)

There is certainly the tone of the swansong about these observations. Patrick has lost his brother as well as his good
friend Johnny in the course of a few months and realises that
when he and his generation die, there will be nobody to replace them. People might be relocated from Dublin to live in
this rural setting, but they won't be the "same sort of people". Finishing the shed for Ruttledge will mean that there will
at least be some sort of monument to their friendship. In her
Irish Times review of *That They May Face the Rising Sun*, Eileen
Battersby comments that there is a special dynamic at work
in the novel: "Time, and with it life, is passing" (Battersby,
2001). She goes on to conclude that McGahern is "a supreme
chronicler of the ordinary as well as of the closing chapters of
traditional Irish rural life". In this comment, she shows an appreciation of what constitutes McGahern's real literary
achievement in this book.

Let us now consider the novel with these few ideas at the
back of our minds. There is no real plot, no strong central
consciousness to hold our attention. What we have is a community, made up of middle-aged to old inhabitants, whose lives
have not changed significantly for several decades. The houses
may have washing machines and televisions, farming may have
become more mechanised with tractors and bailing machines,
and yet the people are still committed to the traditional ideals,
especially neighbourliness. Jamesie is very much to the fore as
a neighbour. He is fulfilling the *cuairdíocht* tradition of the
1930s, '40s and '50s in Ireland. Hardly a day passes but that he
visits the Ruttledges' house. Joe and Kate Ruttledge met in
London and decided to come to try their hand at farming a
plot of land that they bought along with their present abode

located beside a lake. Jamesie loves to keep abreast of the local gossip, but he is a loyal and true friend to the returned
emigrants, for whom he has genuine affection.

He likes to make fun of the fact that they don't go to
Mass. Joe had been training for the priesthood when he discovered that he didn't have the faith. Jamesie cannot compre-
hend how such an insignificant fact as lack of belief should
prevent the couple from attending Mass: "'I don't believe', he
mimicked. 'None of us believes and we go. That's no bar.'"
(RS, 2). When asked why he goes if he doesn't believe, Jamesie
retorts: "To look at the girls. To see the whole performance.
. . . We go to see all the other hypocrites" (RS, 2). There is a
sense in which local traditions, often pagan in origin, hold
great sway over the community. Fr Conroy is respected as
someone who doesn't interfere too much in the day-to-day
lives of his parishioners. Patrick Ryan offers this assessment:
"Fr Conroy is plain. The priests had this country abulling with
religion once. It's a good job it's easing off" (RS, 82). Later in
the novel, Ryan repeats the same assessment but adds a reference to the emphasis the priests laid on sin: "They had this
whole place abulling with religion once. People were afraid to
wipe their arses with grass in case it was a sin" (RS, 224). This
type of gloomy accentuation of the fallen state of man's nature cannot have been easy to bear. Ryan is certainly glad to
see the back of it.

Fr Conroy is, in fact, one of the most sympathetic por-
trayals of a priest in McGahern's fiction. It's almost as though
this man sees the people for what they are: simple,
neighbourly and yet rebellious when someone attempts to
dictate to them. The local IRA activist, Jimmy Joe McKiernan,
is a publican, auctioneer and the local undertaker. His role and
influence in the local community are almost greater than those
of the priest. That said, Fr Conroy is a man for whom the ag-
nostic Joe Ruttledge has respect. A few months after they returned to live in the area, the priest visited the Ruttledges'

house. He apologised for disturbing them but admitted that
the local bishop had him tormented to find out why Joe
turned his back on the priesthood: "I believe in living and letting live. The man up in Longford [the bishop] is very interested in you and why you left the Church and has me
persecuted about you every time he comes" (*RS*, 66). Discreet
and gentle, although certainly not weak, Fr Conroy blends into
the local countryside and does not believe in excessively rock-
ing the boat of the Lake people. When Jamesie's brother,
Johnny, dies during his annual summer holiday from London,
the priest makes a telling commentary on a generation of Irish
people who were forced to emigrate:

> "These people forced into England through no fault of
> their own were often looked down on — most un-
> justly looked down on — by some whose only good
> was that they managed to remain at home with little
> cause to look down on anybody. It's always the
> meanest and poorest sorts who have the need to
> look down." (*RS*, 295)

This type of statement shows the priest to have the courage
of his convictions when he thinks that harsh truths need to
be stated. He knows the people with whom he shares his life
and ministry: the petty jealousies and rivalries, the tendency
to try to "put down" the neighbours, the rawness and cruelty
that can result from spending your life fighting against nature.

Johnny's life in England began when he fell in love with a
local girl, Anna Mulvey, who was two-timing him with Peadar
Curran, whom she followed to London. When it didn't work
out with Peadar, she began writing to Johnny who readily
dropped everything to go and join her in London. When the
relationship ended and she married someone else, Johnny
stayed on in England and found work in Ford's of Dagenham.
Every summer he came home and stayed a few weeks with
Jamesie and Mary. He declared to those who asked that

everything was "alphabetical" (great) and that it was lovely to be home. Johnny was a skilled marksman with a rifle and could hit a flying bird with ease. Similarly, he was a crack darts player. On the eve of his death, which takes place during one of his visits home, Ruttledge brings him to the local pub where he observes with surprise Johnny's superb coordination of hand and eye as he effortlessly throws the darts. Some hours later, he is dead.

Ruttledge is asked by Jamesie to lay out the corpse. It is a spiritual experience for him and constitutes one of the key moments in the book:

> The rectum absorbed almost all of the cotton wool. The act was as intimate and warm as the act of sex. The innate sacredness of each single life stood out more starkly in death than in the whole of natural life. To see him naked was also to know what his character and clothes had disguised — the wonderful physical specimen he had been. (RS, 273)

Patrick Ryan, who is usually the person asked to prepare the corpse, arrives late and expresses his dissatisfaction with the job done by Ruttledge and asks: "Why didn't you wait for me, lad? Were you that greedy to get stuck in?" (RS, 277). Once more, we see the roughness that is typical of Ryan's character, a roughness that can sometimes obscure the kind side of his nature. When reflecting on his experience, Ruttledge explains to Kate: "It made death and the fear of death more natural" (RS, 279). The strong pagan element present in the lakeside community is evident in the way in which they choose to bury Johnny. Patrick Ryan says something that explains the title of the book: "He sleeps with his head to the west . . . So that when he wakes he may face the rising sun . . . We look to the resurrection of the dead" (RS, 282). The local clergy would prefer the head to face the church, but local custom prevails.

There is a sense in which the community go their own way in terms of religious observance. They seem to get spiritual sustenance from their proximity to nature (despite the struggles they have to endure because of it) and their relationships with each other. At times of death, they rally round in a way that is similar to what happens in *An tOileánach*. Ó Criomthain's islanders drop everything when asked to travel to the mainland to get a doctor or a priest. When speaking of the death of a good neighbour, the narrator says: "That was the last end of the grey woman opposite, and I can tell you that, if it wasn't my luck to be rich the day she left the world, it wasn't for want of her good wishes. I hadn't a thing to say against her" (Ó Criomhthain, 2000: 91). There is a fortitude and stoicism in Ó Criomhthain's descriptions of death that are exceptional. He describes the death of his wife and six children in two short paragraphs, without revealing any raw emotion. Similarly, when he tells of how his eldest boy died tragically when he fell off a cliff face, he says what a comfort it was that there was no wound or blemish on any part of his body. Rather than dwelling on his pain, he simply says: "Well, those that pass cannot feed those that remain, and we, too, had to put out our oars again and drive on" (Ó Criomhthain, 2000: 186). The stoicism of paganism is blended into Christian acceptance.

There is something approaching an unwritten set of laws that governs the actions of the people in both *That They May Face the Rising Sun* and *An tOileánach*. Ruttledge is surprised one day, as he walks in the village, at how few people are wearing ash on Ash Wednesday:

> He remembered when everybody in this town would have worn the mark of earth on their foreheads, and if they failed to attend church would have thumbed their own foreheads in secret with the wetted ash of newspapers. (*RS*, 232)

Although very traditional in their approach to life and religion, the characters in this book also show how change has reached into the rural communities of the north west midlands. Technology is beginning to have an impact, as the newly erected telephone poles that obscure the view of the lake illustrate at the end of the book. Apart from the diminished importance of organised religion and the all-pervasive influence of modernity, there is much about the setting and the people that hasn't changed for generations.

Ruttledge's uncle, known affectionately as "The Shah", is a man who belongs to a group of people whose "culture was that of the church and the family" (RS, 236). He is another example of a dwindling breed. A highly successful businessman, he chose the life of a bachelor, probably aware of the fact that he was too set in his ways to ever share his life with another human being: "Where he blossomed was in the familiar and habitual, which he never left willingly. The one aberration of his imaginative shrewdness was a sneaking regard for delinquents, . . . as they tested and gave two fingers to the moral world" (RS, 36). You can see how the rebellious side of The Shah is never far from a conventional surface. He is awkward in his dealings with his long-time assistant, Frank Dolan, with whom he rarely talks and yet to whom he wants to sell his business. His nephew has to organise a loan for Frank and smooth out all the potential problems in order for the deal to go through — the other two men refuse to speak to each other about the sale. Ruttledge is fond of his uncle and appreciates the support the latter gave him when he left the priesthood. This happened at a time when the prevailing climate had been one of accusation and reproach: "Let them go to hell" (RS, 39) was The Shah's reaction and he offered Ruttledge money to continue his studies if he so desired.

When you finish this novel, you are sad to leave behind this wonderful array of characters and the beautiful setting where you have had the privilege of spending a year in their company. Each character has his or her unique function in the community. For example, McGahern gives a prominent role to Bill Evans, the product of an orphanage and industrial school who, when he reached a certain age, was hired out as a glorified slave to a local farm. Bill is a reminder of the great injustice that visited many Irish women who, for various reasons, were forced to give up their children and sometimes ended up in places like the Magdalene Laundries. McGahern chronicles the path followed by Bill:

> His kind was now almost as extinct as the corn-crake. He had fled to his present house from the farm he first worked on. When he was fourteen years old he had been sent out from the religious institutions to that first farm. (RS, 9)

Ruttledge's first encounter with Bill took place when the poor man had been left locked outside his house on a bitterly cold day and had no option other than to go to his neighbour and ask for something to eat. Ruttledge is sympathetic to Bill's plight but also aware of the fact that there is not much he can do to change it. He remembers an incident he witnessed with a boy from a similar background to Bill's who worked as a "skivvy" in the college he attended. One day when serving food in the refectory, he slipped and splashed food on the soutane of a particularly nasty Dean. The priest showed no mercy:

> The beating was sudden and savage. Nobody ate a morsel at any of the tables while it was taking place. . . . Many who had sat mutely at the tables during the beating were to feel all of their lives that they had taken part in the beating through their self-protective silence. (RS, 11)

Bill Evans is fortunate in that he is accepted by the Ruttledges and the others in the community from whom he scrounges cigarettes and food. Even though he is poorly treated by the family in whose care he has been placed, he is fiercely loyal to them. Having reached middle-age, he doesn't like to dwell in the past. When Ruttledge interrogates him on the events of his life, he is promptly told: "Stop torturing me" (*RS*, 12). He later realises that this is the only way that Bill can deal with what has happened to him:

> Bill Evans could no more look forward than he could look back. He existed in a small closed circle of the present. Remembrance of things past and dreams of things to come were instruments of torture. (*RS*, 167)

There are some like Jamesie who suggest that Bill is probably as happy as anyone in the community, and this could well be true. There is a sense in which everyone looks out for him. For example, Ruttledge and Fr Conroy collaborate to ensure that he is supplied with a home in a new housing development in the town. The priest visits Ruttledge to discuss the move and there is a touch of caution in his tone as he ponders on whether Bill will now be happy:

> "Sometimes I think it may be better to let these mistakes run their course. Attempting to rectify them at a late stage may bring in more trouble than leaving them alone". (*RS*, 244–5)

Bill seems content enough as he heads off to the estate. He is not someone who is given to introspection or self-pity. He lives in the present and is happy when he has plenty of food and cigarettes. He is a likeable and convincing character.

Less so is John Quinn, a man who is full of paradoxes. Silver-tongued in his dealings with others, adored by the children of his first marriage, he has a ruthless and sadistic streak when it comes to women. Greatly fascinated by what Jamesie refers to as the "boggy hollow", John Quinn married a young woman who was heiress to "limestone fields and a house and place to

walk into" (RS, 26). He treated her and her parents abomina-
bly. When they arrived back from the church for the wedding
reception, which was organised to take place in her house, he
brought his bride for a walk to the nearby hill where, in full
view of the wedding guests, he claimed his conjugal rights: "He
lifted the blue dress up over her head and put her down on the
blanket. The screech she let out would put your heart cross-
ways" (RS, 28). The guests, embarrassed for the bride's parents, a gentle couple who doted on their daughter, cannot get
away quickly enough after this shocking episode. John Quinn
embodies one of the few unsavoury aspects of the novel. What
he was doing on the hill was asserting to his wife and her family
that he was the boss now. He is unwholesome in his tireless
pursuit of sexual encounters. When his first wife dies and his
children have grown up and left home, he manages to find a
second wife. However, this does not last long, for reasons he
explains in the following manner: "What God intended men
and women to do she had no taste for. What was meant to be
happy and natural was for her a penance" (RS, 23).

After this failed marriage, he regularly has women to stay
in his house. He insists on bringing them to the church and
sitting in the front pew, almost defying Fr Conroy to call him
to task. News of his forthcoming third wedding to a woman
he met thanks to the marriage bureau in Knock sends ripples
of excitement around the inhabitants of the houses beside the
lake. When he insists on bringing the woman to the bridal
suite before the wedding breakfast, there is much conjecture
among the guests as to what is happening. The earthiness of
some of the men is clear from their comments:

> "Maybe she's just dying for the hog," Patrick Ryan said
> provocatively, coarsely. . . .
>   "It's better for herself if she wants it," Jamesie said
> quietly. "Whether she likes it or not, she'll have to
> open the door."

> "She'll get the rod," Bill Evans said suddenly. (*RS*, 168)

The men betray a grudging admiration for John Quinn, whose sexual activities clearly excite their interest. In some of McGahern's earlier fiction, it is possible that John Quinn would have been the central character. His easy charm and elegant turn of phrase succeed in seducing many women, but the last of his brides leaves him soon after the wedding. He wistfully recalls the short time they spent together to Jamesie: "It was like going in and out of a most happy future" (*RS*, 175).

There are many superb characters in *That They May Face the Rising Sun*, but what will ensure the ongoing success of this novel is the way in which it manages to capture for eternity the rituals and customs of a rural Ireland that may not survive another few decades of globalisation. The characters are people with whom it is easy to identify — they are closer to us than Ó Criomhthain's are. Just as is the case with *An tOileánach*, however, we get the strong sense of McGahern's being the chronicler of a dying breed. We have already noted some references to that fact.

Nature is not exempt from the danger of extermination either. The lake's comforting presence is a constant throughout and the rituals of working the land, visiting neighbours, sharing the sparse pieces of news, are all captured with a skill that demonstrates that McGahern is now at the summit of his art. Take the following extract as an example:

> The night and the lake had not the bright metallic beauty of the night Johnny had died: the shapes of the great tree were softer and brooded even deeper in their mysteries. The water was silent, except for the chattering of the wildfowl, the night air sweet with the scents of the ripening meadows, thyme and clover and meadowsweet, wild woodbine high in the whitethorns

> mixed with the scent of wild mint crawling along the
> gravel on the edge of the water. (*RS*, 296)

In another fifty years, this passage will prove invaluable to
anyone who desires to experience what the Irish rural landscape was like towards the end of the twentieth century. The
likelihood is that it will have been greatly transformed in the
intervening period.

John McGahern, in his article on *An tOileánach*, made the
point that Ó Criomhthain did not provide much description
of the island:

> Places are seen in their essential outline, which is in-
> separable from their use or function. . . . A strand is
> there to be crossed, a sea to be fished, a town to be
> reached, a shore to be gained, walked upon, lived
> upon. These are all near and concrete realities, but so
> stripped down to their essentials because of the ne-
> cessities of the action as to seem free of all local
> characteristics. (McGahern, 1987: 8)

McGahern himself describes in far greater detail the
countryside he holds dear. This could be because his characters have time to reflect on the landscape; they do not have
to struggle with nature to the same extent as the islanders
did in order to survive. McGahern shows how sensitive they
are to nature. For example, this is the image evoked when
Ruttledge and Jamesie have finished cutting the hay:

> When all the meadows were cut they looked won-
> derfully empty and clean, the big oak and ash trees in
> the hedges towering over the rows of cut grass, with
> the crows and the gulls descending in a shrieking rab-
> ble to hunt frogs and snails and worms. (*RS*, 106)

The tone is one of celebration and appreciation. It is clear
that McGahern knows the scene he is depicting intimately,
just as he knows the people who inhabit it. We get many ref-

erences to birds, the lake, animals of all sorts, trees and foli-
age. Only someone who has lived for many years in close
proximity to nature, as McGahern has, could capture the
countryside in the way that he does.

Equally, he is adept at delineating the behaviour of his
characters. This is evident in the scene where Jamesie and his
wife, Mary, are faced with the announcement by Johnny of his
plan to come home to live permanently by the lake. Mary is
attached to Johnny but even his annual trips home for the
summer holidays are a strain on both herself and her husband:

> They could not live with him and they could not be
> seen — in their own eyes or in the eyes of others —
> to refuse him shelter or turn him away. The timid,
> gentle manners, based on a fragile interdependence,
> dealt in avoidances and obfuscations. Edges were sof-
> tened, ways found round harsh realities. What was
> unspoken was often far more important than the
> words that were said. Confrontation was avoided
> whenever possible. (*RS*, 186)

This is as good an example as I can find of a writer who is
at home with his material. He "knows" his people and can see
how the mores of the local community weigh heavily on
them. Johnny is a member of the family and, as such, they
couldn't be seen to refuse him a place to live. But the consequences of his moving home would be drastic for all concerned. In the end, Ruttledge writes a letter for his friends in
an attempt to dissuade Johnny from making a decision which
would ultimately be in no one's interest. Fortunately, Johnny
is offered a job as a type of caretaker for the block of flats in
which he lives and so the move never becomes a reality.
While its shadow hung over Mary and Jamesie, however, it
was a source of much disquiet. Eamon Sweeney describes this
passage as "magnificent with its anthropological exactitude"

(Sweeney, 2002: 98) — yet another critic who refers to anthropology in relation to McGahern's work.

We have already seen some of the beautiful evocations of nature, the strong bond that exists between the people, the slow pace of life that allows for a glass of Power's or a cup of tea when a neighbour drops in, the joy of getting good prices for cattle and sheep, the majesty of a man's body as he lies naked in death. There is much philosophising about life also. We have noted how Patrick Ryan is often incisive in his comments. One day he gets Ruttledge to drive him to visit his brother Edmund, who is dying in hospital. He insists on waking the sick man so that he can say to people that he spoke to him before he died — this annoys Ruttledge. On the way home, he comes up with another of his gems: "It'd make you think, lad," Patrick said sourly. "There's not a lot to it when it all comes down" (*RS*, 48). There is great economy of expression in these lines that capture an essential truth. Patrick is not a man to dwell excessively on the dark side of life and yet he is imbued with an understanding that we are but transient beings on this earth. Although Ruttledge is a good friend of his, Patrick does not even go to the bother of alerting him to Edmund's death, and Ruttledge is sad to have missed the funeral. He is also angry at Jamesie for not telling him the news. The unwritten laws that bind this community are sometimes transgressed, especially when people fail to take on board the sensibilities of others. But, of course, Ruttledge is different: they accept him but he is never really one of them, and death brings out that difference.

We know how Ruttledge's lack of faith prevents him from attending Mass and religious services. Nevertheless, he is undoubtedly a deeply spiritual man. One evening, after having spent a lovely day in the company of Mary and Jamesie, he wonders if he is experiencing perfect happiness. He quickly dismisses the thought:

> As soon as the thought came to him, he fought it
> back, blaming the whiskey. The very idea was as dan-
> gerous as presumptive speech: happiness could not be
> sought or worried into being, or even fully grasped; it
> should be allowed its own slow pace so that it passes
> unnoticed, if it ever comes at all. (RS, 183)

Ruttledge is McGahern's mouthpiece in the novel. Like him, he is the friendly but detached observer, the "seer", the prophet. His insights are born out of a carefully nurtured vision of existence that is anchored in the local but reaches the universal.

The speech patterns of the characters are restricted to "a telegraphic minimum", another trait which, according to Declan Kiberd, he shares with Ó Criomhthain (Kiberd, 2000: 535). McGahern certainly has a good ear for local speech patterns and sayings. Every time that Jamesie comes to visit, there is a repetition of the same type of refrain, as he castigates Kate and Joe for not speaking ill of their neighbours. Patrick Ryan stops work and says: "I'm away with myself out to the orchard to cut a button" (RS, 71), a wonderful way of describing a bodily function. The dialogue is full of such richness of language and local dialect, spoken by real people. Johnny and Patrick Ryan discuss how Joe and Kate have managed to keep afloat with the farming, when they are so ill-suited to the task. Patrick observes: "There's an old Shorthorn they milk for the house that would nearly sit in an armchair and put specs on to read the *Observer*" (RS, 76), a comment that betrays a certain bias against people for whom farming is a sort of pastime.

There is a great mixture of emotion and exactitude in this chronicle of the lives of a rural community who share joys and sorrow, wonder and awe, and who are brought close by their sense of living out the last moments of a culture. In his *Irish Classics*, Declan Kiberd mentions how in the Blasket autobiographies by Ó Criomhthain, Peig Sayers and Muiris Ó Súilleabháin, the island culture achieved "an extraordinary concentration of utterance" that comes from their being doomed to pass away. "In each book, something of the tradition survived the lament for its passing", and he concludes by remarking:

> All were, in that sense, examples of the energizing effect of a real homage to past culture: for in each text a deep humility before that tradition is accompanied by an invincible pride, and both characteristics shine through the pages. The islanders are scarcely part of the literate world, yet they speak a kind of elegant poetry. They live in a sort of socialist commune, where all share a common danger and poverty, yet they bear themselves with the beautiful reserve and considered manners of real aristocrats. (Kiberd, 2000: 520–1)

Such comments apply equally to *That They May Face the Rising Sun* (and to a lesser extent to *Amongst Women*), which is McGahern's tribute to his rural Ireland and its inhabitants. His essay on *An tOileánach* contains a comment that captures an essential ingredient of his most recent novel: "I think that the strange sense of timelessness that the book has, of being outside time, comes from the day, a single day breaking continually over the scene and the action" (McGahern, 1987: 9). This seamless, timeless quality is what gives *That They May Face the Rising Sun* its power and universality.

When Mary gazes on her son and his wife, she wonders:

> . . . how so much time had disappeared and emerged again in such strange and substantial forms that were not her own. Across her face there seemed to pass many feelings and reflections: it was as if she ached to touch and gather in and make whole those scattered years of change. But how can time be gathered in and kissed? There is only flesh. (*RS*, 125)

This is one of the few references to family in *That They May Face the Rising Sun*. *Amongst Women* was about a family in the throes of change. Mary's nostalgia at the passage of time that is beyond her comprehension is conveyed with the minimum amount of fuss and the maximum efficiency. She does not enjoy a close relationship with her daughter-in-law, who is ambitious for her husband, but she gets much joy from her grandchildren when they come to visit. Like the numerous clocks in her house which are out of sync, she is incapable of controlling time. She is not prone to dwelling unduly on the past, but there are moments like the one above when she cannot avoid marvelling at how quickly time has gone.

Writing about how people voted in A Novel Choice, Shane Hegarty emphasised how deeply McGahern's latest novels, in particular, have influenced the Irish reader: "Perhaps most striking is the impact John McGahern's novels have made on the Irish novel. Apart from *Amongst Women* finishing third, had *That They May Face the Rising Sun* been included on the original list, it may have polled very well. There are many people who believe the book to be an instant classic" (Hegarty: 2003, 11). People have been moved by the most recent novel's evocation of a passing world and it received three times as many "votes" as any other novel that readers felt should be included. It all reinforces the point made at the beginning of this chapter when I said that McGahern's chronicling of the closing chapters of rural Ireland marks him as a writer who is admired and revered for encapsulating a civilisation whose demise is near.

Conclusion

John McGahern's journey began with a minor classic, *The Barracks*, which preceded the banning of *The Dark*, when he was the recipient of unwanted publicity and shame. He then moved through the experimental years when he was writing *The Leavetaking* and *The Pornographer*, two novels that received mixed reactions from the critics. His collections of short stories during the 1970s and 1980s kept McGahern's name in the public domain and confirmed his feel for his chosen material. Finally, he achieved spectacular success with *Amongst Women* and *That They May Face the Rising Sun*, a success that, because it has been so slow and painful in coming, must now be savoured all the more by the writer.

The wait has been worthwhile: few now contest the canonical stature McGahern has attained in Irish and world fiction. Some go so far as to speak of him as the next Irish Nobel laureate for literature. If he were to attain that accolade, would it not show how he conforms to the paradigm of the Irish writer who initially was not accepted in his own country but ended up being accepted because he captured something so deeply ingrained in all of us? Declan Kiberd once more supplies a telling evaluation:

> People first of all shuddered and then they realised:
> "My God, he has told our innermost story." . . . I
> think people have that feeling when they read McGa-
> hern: in some way the histories of their own families
> has been told with a kind of tenderness and honesty
> and a mixture of wistfulness and longing, that is ap-
> propriate to the experience. So they actually feel rati-
> fied by him, they who refused once to ratify him.
> (Maher and Kiberd, 2002: 93)

We live in a period of uncertainty and globalisation. Contemporary Ireland and the Ireland depicted by McGahern
would appear at first to be poles apart. A steady rise in GDP
and GNP, excessive abuse of alcohol and drugs among both
young and old, continuing threats to our cultural specificity
and environment, the breakdown of family life, corruption
among some of our politicians and business leaders, clerical
child abuse, the impact of modernity on our country: these
are the sort of issues that dominate the media at the beginning of the third millennium. The Church and State, for so
long the pillars of the state that was established in 1922, are
in apparent decline. With such uncertainty about the future, it
is more important than ever to have writers like John McGahern who reveal to us from whence we have come and
where we may be headed. His local scenes, sketched with
such precision and charm, supply a canvas which the vast ma-
jority of Irish people can recognise. His popularity is not in
any way confined to the older generation — he has readers
among almost every age group — or to his native country. In
recent times, he has become a truly international figure in the
world of fiction. He offers us a glimpse of what is best and
worst about Ireland and its people. From his home in Fox-
field, County Leitrim, he produces a wonderful depiction of
an Ireland that is resistant to the inroads of modernity. Like
Seamus Heaney and Brian Friel, he manages to transmit the

local voice in a way that makes Ardcarne and Oakport as familiar and, more importantly, as interesting as Dublin, Belfast or Limerick. The scenes and characters he portrays are not confined to any one place or time. They have the universal qualities that McGahern recognises and to which he gives a literary embodiment. The novelist Colm Toibín maintains that McGahern has been enormously successful "in that he has established the notion of a small place becoming a whole world and sticking to that throughout a writing life without in any way lessening the power of his work" (quoted in Wroe, 2002). In these few words, Toibín explains McGahern's huge success while at the same time justifying the title of this book.

Appendix

An Interview with John McGahern

This interview was conducted on 22 August 2002.

EM: John, thank you for agreeing to do this interview. I know that you have a particular admiration for a few Irish writers, most notably Ernie O'Malley and Tomás Ó Criomhthain. What is it exactly that you admire about them?

JMG: Well, I admire many Irish writers, Yeats particularly, Joyce, Beckett, Synge, people like George Moore, Carleton, Michael McLaverty, Corkery, Kavanagh — I don't like lists or league tables of writers I enjoy. I admire these writers because they write well and they're all different. I like Mairtín Ó Cadhain. Ó Criomhthain's *The Islandman* is a remarkable book. It can be seen in Paolo Vivante's remarkable *The Homeric Imagination* that while Ó Criomhthain is no Homer, the same sort of laws apply to the material, to the way of seeing and thinking. This can also be seen in E.R. Dodds' book, *The Greeks and the Irrational.*

EM: In the Homeric book, you have this solitary, epical figure that reminds one of Ó Criomhthain, struggling to save a civilisation that is on the verge of extinction.

JMG: Yes, but all civilisations are disappearing, all civilisations are to a certain extent artificial and there's nothing going to be so out of fashion as that which is most present. Tradition, when all is said and done, is civilisation, which needs to be continually renewed and revitalised; and what proves to be good or useful in the new will become part of tradition. Fashion, which is begotten from the desire to change — Proust articulated this — is quick to change itself. In modern literature, people who demand change are often just demanding trendiness. A writer, by getting his words right, by writing well, will reflect everything his work is capable of reflecting, including the political. This is especially true of the novel. The novel, I believe, is the most social of all art forms, as it is the most closely allied to the idea of manners and an idea of society. To a certain extent, all true novels are shaped differently because the content of a novel, I think, more than any other art form, decides its form. I think O'Malley's *On Another Man's Wound* is a marvellously vivid book. These books reflect their time, but parts of the time they reflect is now part of our own time, in the sense that it would be a shallow present that didn't contain the past. The novel can never be abstract, and for this reason the "art" novel is a nonsense in the same way as the abstract novel is, because as soon as a person utters a sentence or has a thought, or is said to have a thought, it immediately identifies him in a particular place and in a particular time.

EM: You've stolen my thunder for my second question in a sense. I have been trying to develop a theory which reckons that your most recent novel, *That They May Face the Rising Sun*, has a haunting quality that leads me back to Ó Criomhthain's *The Islandman*. The reader has the distinct impression that this is a swansong to a civilisation that is on the verge of extinction, just like the Blasket Islands of Ó Criomhthain's account. Would that be a fair assessment?

JMG: Well, I'm only writing in the same way as I've always written. But there is a theory — I don't know whether it's true or not — that often at the end of a particular cycle, as a society falls away, it becomes utterance. You could say Ó Criomhthain is an example of that type of swansong in the same way that Yeats produces the swansong of Anglo-Irish civilisation, which, to a certain extent, he also invented. If a writer only sets out to reflect a particular society he will only be of interest to a historian or a sociologist. What is permanent is the spirit or the personality in language, the style, and that's what lasts. A book that was written two hundred years ago can be as alive today as it was when it was first published, and last month's novel can be as dead in a year as a laboratory mouse. I do think that if a person gets his words right that he will reflect many things; but if he sets out deliberately to do it, he'll be writing journalism. To a certain extent, Kavanagh comes out of a society that was at an end as well. The main reason Kavanagh is read today is for the liveliness and the spirit and the truth of the language. When he's bad, as he often is, he's bad like nobody else: he's outrageously bad. You know that poem by Auden on the death of Yeats: "Time that is as ignorant in a week to a beautiful physique / Pardons language and forgives / Everything by which it lives."

EM: In the Preface to the second edition of *The Leavetaking*, you acknowledge that in the first published draft you had been "too close to the 'Idea', and the work lacked that distance, that inner formality or calm, that all writing, no matter what it is attempting, must possess". Do you think that the same comment could apply equally well to *The Dark*? Do your subsequent novels come closer to achieving the distance of which you spoke in 1974?

JMG: Well I don't know. I can tell you how that happened. *The Leavetaking* was written around an idea: there is the "I", the first person singular, and the Other which is the beloved or Otherest. The "I" generally expresses itself in the language of lyricism or love, while basically the language of love should belong to the other, the object of love. But, in fact, our knowledge of the other comes to us in reportage. I was trying in that novel to write the first half lyrically and then to write the second half journalistically and to see if the two things could be married or joined at the end. I felt, rightly or wrongly, that it hadn't worked, that it was probably impossible anyhow. My work began to have some success in France and I was friendly with the translator and poet, Alain Delahaye. I asked him when he was working on the translation if he minded if I had another go at the second part, and then rewrote it for Alain's translation. I did it for myself, to have another go at the idea. That was how Faber heard about it and asked to see it; and when they decided that they wanted to go with the second version, they asked me to write the Preface. That's how that came to be written.

EM: When I was reading through the Preface, I was a bit confused about a number of issues. One part in particular caused me problems: "It was an attempt to reflect the purity of feeling with which all the remembered 'I' comes to us, the banal and the precious alike; and yet how that more than 'I' — the beloved, the "otherest", the most trusted moments of that life — stumbles continually away from us as poor reportage, and to see if these disparates could in any way be made true to one another." The remembered "I" brought to mind Wordsworth's *Tintern Abbey* ("emotion recollected in tranquility"). Memory is a big issue in *The Leavetaking*.

JMG: One of my favourite definitions of art is that it abolishes time and establishes memory and, if you reflect on it, you couldn't have the image without memory. The image is at the base of the imagination and it's the basic language of writing.

EM: When you're too close to the "Idea" then, that impacts a bit on how you report it.

JMG: For some reason or other — there's an awful lot of confusion about this — a work of art has to conform to certain laws, and it's been my experience that I've made my worst artistic mistakes by keeping too close to what happened. For some reason, even when what happens by accident is close to the way you see it in work, it still needs to be re-ordered, reinvented in order to be true. In a very simple way, one of the differences between life and writing is that writing has always to be believable, whereas much of what goes on in life doesn't. Also, without the difficulty of having to reinvent, language loses tension. It's like what I often say about escapism, a lot of what goes on in art is escaping into reality and a lot of what happens in life is completely artificial, an escape into convention. Just on that question of prefaces, I'm writing the preface to two novels by an American writer I admire, John Williams. I showed them to Caroline Michel at Vintage. She loved them, but said that as it was I who was the cause of her buying them, and as they're unknown, I'd have to write the prefaces, which was the last thing I wanted to do. John Williams is a superb prose stylist and his novels are all different on the surface. They could be the work of four different novelists. His method is to go as far as possible from the self and towards the other, and then find his way back through the self. He writes about the Roman Empire, he writes about a buffalo hunt, and in his novel, *Stoner*, he writes about an obscure university professor. He says in *Stoner*: "Like all lovers, they spoke much of one another as if thereby they would understand the world that brought them into being." It's deliciously ironical and playful. "Thereby" is a very interesting word there, how it is placed.

EM: Williams is picking subjects, he's almost reinventing himself with each novel.

JMG: Yes. In the Introduction he wrote to his classic edition of English Renaissance Poetry, he said of Ben Jonson "It is, finally, a language that has passed from the starkness and bareness of outer reality through the dark, luxuriant jungle of the self, and has emerged from that journey entire and powerful" — and he might just as well have been writing about his own prose. I mean, does that give any kind of an answer to your question? Hardy always refers to the "Otherest" or the "Thou" as the beloved.

EM: I struggled with that sentence when I was writing the chapter on *The Leavetaking* and you've certainly cleared up that point for me. Moving on to other things, one of my personal favourites among your various books is *The Pornographer*. It was an experimental novel that revealed a side of Irish society that you would have expected to shock a lot more people than *The Dark* did. And yet it caused far less fuss than your second novel. Do you think that says anything about the evolution of Irish society in the intervening years?

JMG: I think they were more sophisticated by the time *The Pornographer* was published. I think they learned to ignore the novel rather than to ban it!

EM: And was it ignored? Did it sell badly?

JMG: It sold very badly here. It sold well in France and Italy. They published it in Germany and it didn't sell at all. In fact, they then changed the title to *Love in Winter*.

EM: *Love in Winter*! I'm not surprised it didn't sell well!

JMG: Well, it did much better as *Love in Winter* than as *The Pornographer*. Again, rightly or wrongly, what I was trying to do in *The Leavetaking*, as in *The Pornographer*, was almost impossible. *The Pornographer* was a deliberate attempt to see could sex be written about. The reason that the main character is so uninteresting is that this obsession with sexuality is enervating. He falls into that disease, which is a very Irish malaise, that since all things are meaningless it makes no difference what you do, and best of all is to do nothing. In this way he causes as much trouble to himself and to others as if he had set out deliberately to do evil. Basically, that is what I was after. I had never read pornography before and I had to read some of it in order to write about it. it. Some of it is remarkably badly written and quite comic without intending to be. There was a selection of magazines near the bus station when I was teaching in Newcastle. Basically, it was a very old theory I was working on: You can trace the progress of the sun better by examining the dust or the shade than by looking directly up into the sky. So the pornography was a kind of backdrop to see if the sexuality, in its vulnerability and its humanness, could be written about. My own feeling is that it probably can't.

EM: And it marks a kind of experimental phase.

JMG: I suppose. I don't think I could have gone on and written *Amongst Women* or the other books if I hadn't written *The Pornographer*.

EM: It contains a lot of profound philosophical statements and insights. The narrator is both likeable and despicable. He's loving and yet he's detached. At the end of the novel when he declares that "by not paying attention" he had caused untold damage, he achieves a certain insight into his own character. He also sees the possibility for a happier future for himself by choosing to go back to live on a farm in the west. He is the first of your characters to voluntarily choose to go back to his rural roots.

JMG: The novels never leave the country after that. *The Pornographer* was nearly made into a film a couple of times and I wrote a script for it. I set it in a porno factory near Connolly Station. The pornographers are making videos while pretending to promote tourism — they use an aeroplane for filming much of the pornography, arriving at airports, leaving from airports — and then they look for an Arts Council grant. A Pádraig Flynn type is the Minister for Culture, and when he arrives in the factory, they wheel away the aeroplane (their logo) and they get out a curragh and they have girls at spinning wheels. They're supposedly exporting this stuff abroad to advertise the Ireland of the Welcomes. Like a lot of film scripts, it never got made, but it was nearly made a couple of times. There is an Italian director interested now. Whether he'll ever do anything about it or not I don't know. As Larkin suggests, money, plainly, has something to do with life, and even more so when it comes to making movies.

EM: I could imagine how a French film producer, if the Italian project doesn't materialise, would be comfortable with that type of material. I think the reason why the novel appealed to the French is a result of the philosophical undercurrents that are there. I don't think Irish people in general have the philosophical grounding that permits them to fully understand some of the issues at the heart of the novel.

JMG: Well, that's not for me to say. The French saw *The Pornographer* as a black comedy.

EM: It was compared to Camus's *The Stranger*. Have you ever read *The Stranger*?

JMG: I have — I admired the novel, especially the first part. I don't think the second part works. It is probably Camus's best novel.

EM: Again, in terms of atmosphere, Meursault, the main character in Camus's novel, is one of those people who won't toe the line and who's indifferent to public opinion.

JMG: I've always liked Camus's evocations of places. Some of his essays on Algiers are marvellous.

EM: Meursault has it also, this sense of place. When he is in prison, he misses the sea and the sun terribly, the smell of Marie's hair, walking in the streets.

JMG: And you can't forget that old people's home where his mother dies. The funeral and all that. The mother's old lover taking shortcuts through the fields in order to keep up with the cortège.

EM: I agree with you. I think there's a great strength to the first part. It was probably impossible to maintain that right through to the end.

JMG: It's almost like an idea, the second part.

EM: Do you have any theory as to your popularity in France? *The Barracks* featured on their *agrégation* course (a type of taught PhD).

JMG: I think a lot of popularity, a lot of everything, is down to luck. I think a book can come out at a certain time and be successful and come out at another time and fall flat.

EM: John, is there any one of your works of which you are especially proud? Certainly, *Amongst Women* is deservedly rated as being an Irish classic. Is it your favourite or do you have one?

JMG: The writer is, I think, a dangerous person to ask about his books. You are always most closely connected to your last book. I'd have to say, for that reason, that I prefer *That They May Face the Rising Sun* to *Amongst Women*. But then again I would have probably said the same thing about *Amongst Women* after I wrote it. I like something Rilke said: "There are certain books that must long for the death of their author so that they assume their own lives." I think that when a writer finishes a book, he has dealt in images and rhythms, and out of the material the book is shaped finally — the last thing a writer does is shape it — and once he does that, it will not live again until it finds a reader. It will have as many different lives as it will have readers. No two readers will read it the same. After that, I think that the novelist, in the sense of manners and common sense, is out of it. That is why I'd say he is the least reliable person to talk about it. He knows the mechanics and various things like that but he probably knows less about its overall effect than a reader. Writers are never asked to judge their own books. I think there's too much made of the romantic notion of the writer. Each person has a private world — and I've said this several times — that others cannot see. The only difference between the writer and the reader is that the writer has a certain gift or talent that enables him to dramatise that private world. But it's with another's private world that a book is animated, that it's brought to life in reading. I think that the whole of literature would collapse without the solitary reader. No matter how people try to legislate for literature with university courses, with prizes, with reviews, it still all comes down to the solitary reader being king and queen. You never know what the reader is going to come up with. And if somebody likes a book, it may be because of a fresh insight that the author never dreamed of. A book only lives if it finds lovers. Lovers talk. I used to fight against the whole idea around the artist because I don't like the idea of the mystique around the artist. I don't think writing has anything to do with intelligence — though intelligence certainly helps no matter what task you undertake — and I don't think that any of the psychological laws apply. It is a sort of mystery. It's like having perfect pitch in singing. It's something you're born with and then stumble on, and after that you have to work. It makes all other work seem easy.

EM: I suppose the fact that you feel closest to *That They May Face the Rising Sun* now indicates that as a writer you have moved on. I would imagine that with each novel, a new stage is reached in your artistic development.

JMG: There would be no point in repeating the same thing.

EM: But your style is being chiselled down. It is very finely honed in *That They May Face the Rising Sun*.

JMG: That's not for me to say. People have said that they took pleasure in reading the book slowly and were reluctant to finally leave the world around the lake.

EM: I had the same impression. I didn't want my reading to come to an end because it would mean departing from a community and ambience with which I had become familiar and intimate. John, you mentioned Proust and Flaubert in the course of our previous interview in a way that shows that you agree with aspects of their approach to their art. Are you conscious of your European literary inheritance in any way?

JMG: To a certain extent. I don't think I would have become a writer except I got access to that library where I read everything, including the Zane Grey novels. I read for nothing but pleasure. Books are there to be experienced rather than analysed. It's very dangerous when people start reading what's considered "good literature" because I think pleasure is the least fallible guide to what is good. There comes a time in your reading when it changes and you become conscious that all stories are more or less the same story and that all stories reflect life. Then you read more for the style or the personality through which the story is seen than for the story itself. The quality of writing becomes more important than the material out of which it is shaped. In your earlier years you read for the crude excitement of the story, its suspense. In an essay in which I spoke about this I do say that those books about the Rocky Mountains that I used to devour when I was young had to become *Mansfield Park* if they were to retain my new attention. Having said that, I think that the novel or the story can never exist in a vacuum. There is always the need for the concreteness of a story.

EM: The novel has to be social. But with regard to Proust and Flaubert, I know that you have read them . . .

JMG: I think I've read all of Proust and Flaubert, even *Bouvard and Pécuchet*. I admire *Contre St Beuve* and Flaubert's Letters almost as much as the novels. When you come on criticism like Vivante's and Dodds's and Auden's, you realise how artificial are the divisions between poetry and fiction and criticism. It's just like the class system. My most important book was the Catholic Church. I love the description of the medieval Gothic churches being the bibles of the poor, in the sense that before people could read, the story of Christ was given to them through sculpture and painting. It wasn't ornament. It was a function. At a certain time, I turned to continental writers because what I was looking for was scarce enough in English, particularly in prose.

EM: And of course it didn't just have a European dimension. It also had a world dimension, the Catholic Church.

JMG: It reached Cootehall and Aughawillian anyhow. I think that the eighteenth century had a deep influence on English literature. Religion became an arm of state and it was a sort of bad manners to have religious thoughts in prose. "The proper study of Mankind is Man": that implies that somehow it's bad manners to deal with the mystery of existence. I see morals as being our relationships with each other and religion is our relationship with all that surrounds our life. I see the two as completely separate though the Church wouldn't see it that way. I don't think it's possible for a writer of my generation born in Ireland to avoid religion, even if it has to be by the path of opposition. It was the dominant force in that society, and, in any sense of the spirit, it was mostly all that was there, even if some of it was unattractive.

EM: Yes, I heard you mention Céline in your interview with Mike Murphy. Céline is an author whom I only came to read lately. I found *Voyage to the End of the Night* powerful in its desperation. It provides a savage indictment of the collapse of all the systems put in place by Western civilisation prior to World War I.

JMG: I used Céline in a comparison with Kavanagh, where they're both speaking about the same thing. They provide opposite statements and they are equally valid: it depends on the expression and the personality of the writer. Kavanagh said: "Posterity has no time for anything but the soul." Céline says: "Invoking posterity is like making speeches to maggots."

This statement, while savage, is as spiritual in its own way as Kavanagh's. They're both true though they state the opposite.

EM: In Ireland, being an island, you'd expect us to have been isolated but we weren't. We had plenty of links with the Continent. Our priests went abroad to be educated during the Penal times . . .

JMG: Wordsworth is a great religious poet. But religious sentiment was always more tolerated in verse in English than it was in prose. In the great English novels, I always think of them as being completely secular. Jane Austen, George Eliot, even Evelyn Waugh. When Waugh talks about God, he a kind of chief constable to keep the criminal classes in order. *Brideshead Revisited*, which is full of his Catholicism, is his worst book because his touch isn't certain.

EM: Man–woman relationships have a nasty habit of turning out badly in your short stories. There is often one apparently insignificant event that sours everything. The male character in "My Love, My Umbrella" observes: "Through my love it was the experience of my death I was passing through, for the life of the desperate equals the anxiety of death. . . ." What are your views on love and sexuality? Are sex and death connected in your view?

JMG: I don't think that my views would be any more valid on these things than any other person. You can say a couple of things about that. Montherlant said, "Happiness writes white", and I agree with that. Happiness is its own expression. You get Oscar Wilde saying the same thing in a much more general, flamboyant way: "All tragedies end in death and all comedies in marriage!" I believe that happiness is its own expression and only a fool would write out of happiness. For that very same reason I think that one of the consolations of

Heaven, if we ever find ourselves there, will be that there will be no writers in it. There will be no need to write. It's the same with a happy relationship to anything. You enjoy it while you can. Life seems to make sure that we don't go laughing all the time or for very long.

EM: That's why love and death are so closely intertwined?

JMG: In erotic love, Proust captures this exactly when he says that one's own sense of self passes over to the other, and then rejection is like death without the insensibility. "I cannot live without her" runs through all of song. Proust articulated and analysed this when he says that there is no carnal attraction of any profundity that does not contain within itself the seeds of calamity. The sexual need is the strongest natural need after the need for food, in that we have to live through another. "Big job, not easy", a dear uncle of mine used to proclaim with wonderful self-complacency about anything elevated or difficult.

EM: I think you have a sentence in *The Pornographer* that compares the orgasm to our last breath.

JMG: I don't remember. There's a poem, "The Silk Worms", by a New Zealand poet I like, and it ends with this image of the silk worms when they mate: "White moth" — clearly echoing mouth — "White moth moves closer to moth / Lover to lover / There's a pang of joy / On the edge of dying / They dream that they are flying."

EM: That's an extraordinary image. Staying with the short stories for a while, in "Oldfashioned", the young boy who is barred from pursuing a possible career in the British army because of his father's misplaced prejudice, ends up making documentary films about the darker sides of Irish life. We read: "Some thought they were serious, well made and compulsive viewing, bringing things to light that were in bad need of light; but others maintained that they were humourless, morbid, and restricted to a narrow view that was more revealing of private obsessions than any truths about life or Irish life in general." Were these lines written as an ironic commentary on how people had viewed your own work?

JMG: I was being playful, playful or ironic. Those would be some of the things that were said about my work when I was young. I was told that these things I was recounting couldn't happen in Irish society. "Oldfashioned" is an unusual story in that it takes society as a character in very much the same way as Hardy uses the heath or nature, and this is a playful comment about the depiction and how society views itself, or at least that was the intention. It's not meant to be taken too seriously.

EM: As you say though, the world, the hidden Ireland, into which you shone a light has now been exposed.

JMG: I didn't set out to do that. I was just writing in the same way as I am today. I've never written anything that wasn't in my mind for several years and the only reason I write anything down is that it stays in my mind and won't go away until it's written down. And sometimes when it's written down I find there's nothing there in the first place; it disappears, you just throw away what you've written. Other times it becomes work. In prose the material dictates the shape and very soon you'll know, for instance, whether it's going to be a short story or a novel, and at the very end it is given or finds its own individual shape as novel or story. The intensity, the rhythm in the short story would be intolerable in a novel, it would be tiresome after a while. A short story is much closer to a drama or a poem than it is to a novel. If you watch any good short story, it makes one point and one point only. All the drama moves towards one point and away from the same point. It's like a small explosion, and then the reader has to imagine what happened before the story began, and in a way the reader completes the story after it ends. Whereas a novel is a whole, completed world. I think that the short story is often stronger in less structured societies where locality and individualism are rampant, while the novel is stronger in very structured societies like England and France. In America I think that the great American short story writers are probably better writers than the great American novelist (whoever he or she is!). *The Great Gatsby* seems to me to be a great American novel without bearing any pretentious baggage.

EM: You are very close to nature. In *That They May Face the Rising Sun*, the lake, the trees, the birds, the changing seasons are all evoked with precision and tenderness. Does nature provide you with spiritual food?

JMG: No. Not that I'm aware of. We are part of nature, like the animals and the trees, and we are all part of that passing world we learn to love and to leave. Naturally, it is described with care or attention, as everything else should be, and it is also seen through a certain vision, maybe fallible and flawed, but mine, or those of my characters.

EM: The circle is a very strong part of your work. In the appropriately named "Wheels", the son realises that his life is a circle when he sees his frail father dismounting from the tractor, "body that had started my journey to nowhere". You appear to be looking for the perfect circle in your writing also and to be aware that such a quest is of necessity unending?

JMG: I don't think anything really ends, but takes different forms, and almost everything comes round again if we can wait.

EM: Human relationships in *That They May Face the Rising Sun* are of a more harmonious nature than in your other novels. Characters like Jamesie, with his wit and kindness, offer a softer view of human nature. Do you think that this has something to do with the fact that you're mellowing with the passing of the years?

JMG: It would be comforting to think that with all that age and change there's a development in depth and understanding, if not in scope, but that's not for me to say.

EM: The scene of the preparation of Johnny's corpse for the wake is a masterpiece. We read: "The innate sacredness of each single life stood out more darkly in death than in the whole of its natural life." Do you think about death much? Do you believe in the afterlife? Do you see your writing as a spiritual exercise in any way?

JMG: I'm at that age when I'm losing friends and companions. It's impossible *not* to think about it. It's just a fact, like birth. Once you are given life, you are also given a future death. It's always there. Recently, on a train, I heard three biddies who were eating and drinking and gossiping to beat the band, mostly about people who were ill or dying or about to get married; and in the middle of all this, one said, "Isn't it great we can't see around the corner?" I don't mean this in the same way, but I have no interest in an afterlife. I'm only interested in what I know and care about. One of the more uncomfortable facts about growing old is that while you are failing, everything around becomes more interesting, because you know more. One of the hard things about being young is that most of the time you don't know what the hell is going on around you.

EM: How do you react to the assessment posited by Declan Kiberd that you are "the foremost prose writer in English now in Ireland?" Do you have to pinch yourself at times and wonder how public opinion has changed so much since the banning of *The Dark*? Does it make you sceptical of the Irish reading public or is it just the ones who don't read your work and still criticise it that disturb you?

JMG: Certainly, it's more pleasant to be praised than to be censored. I have never seen other writers as rivals. If they are any good, they are themselves and different, and are there to be enjoyed. The real competition is always, I think, with oneself, in my case, with my dislike of work. I never had any quarrel with the public since I believe a writer can only bow. I feel lucky and privileged and honoured that my work is read.

EM: What are your writing plans and ambitions for the next few years?

JMG: No great plans. I'm beginning to work again. What it will become I have no idea at this stage, and it may not become anything at all.

Select Bibliography

Novels, Short Stories and Other Writings by John McGahern

(a) Novels

The Barracks, London: Faber and Faber, 1963; New York: Macmillan, 1964; London: Panther, 1966; London: Quartet, 1977; London: Faber and Faber, 1983.

The Dark, London: Faber and Faber, 1965; New York: Knopf, 1966; London: Panther, 1967; London: Quartet, 1977; London: Faber and Faber, 1983; New York: Penguin, 1983.

The Leavetaking, London: Faber and Faber, 1974; Boston: Little Brown, 1975; London: Quartet Books, 1977.

The Leavetaking, Revised edition, London: Faber and Faber, 1984.

The Pornographer, London: Faber and Faber, 1979; New York: Harper and Row, 1979; London: Quartet; Dublin: Poolbeg, 1980; New York: Penguin, 1983.

Amongst Women, London: Faber and Faber, 1990; New York: Harper and Row, 1990; Harmondsworth: Penguin, 1991.

That They May Face the Rising Sun, London: Faber and Faber, 2002; published under the title *By the Lake* for the American edition (Knopf), 2002.

(b) Short Story Collections

Nightlines, London: Faber and Faber, 1970; Boston: Little Brown, 1971; London: Panther, 1973.

Getting Through, London: Faber and Faber, 1978; London: Quartet; Dublin: Poolbeg, 1979; New York: Harper and Row, 1980.

High Ground, London: Faber and Faber, 1985; New York: Viking, 1987.

The Collected Stories, London: Faber and Faber, 1992 (Includes two new stories: "The Creamery Manager" and "The Country Funeral". Also, a number of the original stories were adapted.)

(c) Drama (Radio, TV, Film, Stage)

"Sinclair", *The Listener*, 81 (18 November 1971), 690–2 (an adaptation of "Why We're Here": BBC Radio 3).

"Swallows", 1975 (an adaptation of the short story of the same name for BBC TV).

"The Sisters", 1978. (TV film of James Joyce's short story, Dir. Stephen Frears).

The Rockingham Shoot, September 1987, BBC/Channel 4.

The Power of Darkness, London: Faber and Faber, 1991 (first performed at the Abbey Theatre, Dublin, 16 October 1991).

(d) Selected Writing by John McGahern

McGahern, John (1968), "The Image: Prologue to a Reading at the Rockefeller University", *The Honest Ulsterman*, 8 (December), 10.

McGahern, John (1987), "An tOileánach / The Islandman", *The Canadian Journal of Irish Studies*, 13 (June), 7–15. Reprinted in *The Irish Review*, 6 (Spring 1989), 55–62.

McGahern, John (1989), "Getting Flaubert's Facts Straight", review of *Flaubert*, by Herbert Lottman, *The Irish Times*, Weekend supplement, 29 April, 8.

McGahern, John (1990), "Dubliners", *James Joyce: The Artist and the Labyrinth*, Ed. Augustine Martin, London: Ryan Publishing. Reprinted in *The Canadian Journal of Irish Studies*, 17 (July 1991a), 31–7.

McGahern, John (1991b), "From a Glorious Dream to Wink and Nod", *The Irish Times*, 3 April.

McGahern, John (1991c), "Me Among Protestants: A Bookish Boyhood", *The New York Times Book Review*, April, 25–7.

McGahern, John (1991d), "The Image" (Revised version), *Canadian Journal of Irish Studies*, 17(1), 12.

McGahern, John (1991e), "The Solitary Reader", *Canadian Journal of Irish Studies*, 17 (July), 19–23.

McGahern, John (1993), "The Church and its Spire", *Soho Square 6* (ed. Colm Tóibín), London: Bloomsbury, 17–27.

McGahern, John (1996a), "In Pursuit of a Single Flame", review of *On Another Man's Wound*, by Ernie O'Malley, *The Irish Times*, Weekend supplement, 17 February, 8.

McGahern, John (1996b), "Reading and Writing", *Irish Writers and their Creative Process*, Ed. Jacqueline Genet and Wynne Hellegouarc'h, Gerrards Cross: Colin Smythe, 103–9.

McGahern, John (1999a), "Whatever You Say, Say Nothing", *The Irish Times*, 26 October, 13.

McGahern, John (1999b), Introduction, *John Butler Yeats: Letters to his Son W.B. Yeats and Others 1869–1922*, Ed. Joseph Hone, London: Faber and Faber, 1–24.

McGahern, John (2001), Introduction, *Island: The Collected Stories*, Alistair McLeod, London: Cape, vii–xiv.

McGahern, John (2002), Introductions, *Stoner, Augustus*, John Williams, London: Vintage Classics.

Interviews and Profiles

Carlson, Julia (1990), *Banned in Ireland: Censorship and the Irish Writer*, London: Routledge, 53–67.

Carty, Ciaran (1978), "John McGahern: 'It would be an Insult to be called an Irish Writer'" (Interview), *Sunday Independent*, 11 June.

Carty, Ciaran (1987), "Out of the Dark" (Interview), *Sunday Tribune*, 6 September, 18.

Carty, Ciaran (1991), "Sex, Ignorance and the Irish" (Interview), *The Sunday Tribune*, 29 September, 27.

Downey, Mary (1990), "Unbearable Darkness of Being", *Sunday Independent*, 6 May, 25–6.

Jackson, Joe (1991), "Tales from the Dark Side", *Hot Press*, 14 November, 18–20.

Johnston, Fred (1985), "John McGahern at Fifty", *Irish Times*, 13 August, 10.

Kennedy, Eileen (1984), "Q & A with John McGahern", *ILS*, 3 (Spring), 40.

Lavery, Brian (2003), "From Rural Ireland, Prose Carved with Precise Simplicity", *New York Times*, 1 May, B1 and B6.

Louvel, Liliane, Giles Ménégaldo and Claudine Verley (1994), "Entretien avec John McGahern", *La Licorne*, Poitiers: UFR Langues Littératures, 17 November, 19–32.

Luby, Tom (1979), "In From the Dark", *Irish Times*, 14 June.

Lynch, Audrey L. (1984), "An Interview with John McGahern", *Books Ireland*, 88, 213.

Maher, Eamon (2001), "Catholicism and National Identity in the Works of John McGahern", *Studies*, 90 (357), (Spring), 70–83.

McGarry, Patsy (1991), "McGahern Emerges from the Dark", *Irish Press*, 7 May, 20.

Murphy, Mike (2001), "John McGahern", *Reading the Future: Irish Writers in Conversation with Mike Murphy*, Ed. Clíodhna Ní Anluain. Dublin: Lilliput.

Ollier, Nicole (1995), "Entretien de John McGahern avec Nicole Ollier", *La Licorne*, Poitiers: UFR Langues Littératures, 55–86.

O'Toole, Fintan (1990), "The Family as Independent Republic", *Irish Times*, Weekend supplement, 13 October, 2.

Sampson, Denis (1991), "A Conversation with John McGahern", *Canadian Journal of Irish Studies*, 17 (July), 13–18.

Wallace, Arminta (1990), "Out of the Dark" (Interview), *Irish Times*, 28 April.

Walsh, John (1990), "Throwing Light on Our Dark Side", *Irish Independent*, 4 May, 6. Also published as "Illuminating the Dark Side of the Irish", *The Sunday Times*, 29 April, H8–H9.

Whyte, James (2002), *History, Myth, and Ritual in the Fiction of John McGahern: Strategies of Transcendence*, New York: The Edwin Mellen Press, 227–35.

Wroe, Nicholas (2002), "Ireland's Rural Elegist", Profile of John McGahern, *The Guardian*, 5 January.

Selected Reviews and Criticism on McGahern's Work

Adams, Alice (1979), Review of *The Pornographer*, *New York Times Book Review*, 2 December, 14.

Amiot, Pascale (1994), "L'enfermement dans *The Barracks*", *Études Irlandaises* (October), 45–64.

Anon. (1963), Review of *The Barracks*, *TLS*, 22 February, 132.

Anon. (1965), "Swotting Out of the Farm" (review of *The Dark*), *TLS*, 13 May, 365.

Anon. (1970), "Ireland Intensified" (review of *Nightlines*), *TLS*, 27 November, 1378.

on. (1983), Review of *The Barracks* and *The Dark*, *TLS*, 18 November, 1294.

Anon. (1993), Review of *The Collected Stories*, *New Yorker*, 18 March.

Anon. (1993), Review of *The Collected Stories*, *Sunday Times*, 7 November.

Arnold, Bruce (1990a), "Rich and Truthful Despair" (review of *Amongst Women*), *Irish Independent*, 12 May.

Arnold, Bruce (1990b), "Amongst Winners", *Irish Independent*, 17 October.

Banville, John (1990a), "To Have is to Hold, and Hate" (review of *Amongst Women*), *Observer* (London), 6 May.

Banville, John (1990b), "In Violent Times" (review of *Amongst Women*), *New York Review of Books*, 6 December, 22–3.

Bataillard, Pascal (1995), "John McGahern's Subdued Modernity" *Études Britanniques Contemporaines* (Université de Paul Valéry), Janvier, 85–100.

Battersby, Eileen (2001), "A Superb Earthly Pastoral" (review of *That They May Face the Rising Sun*), *Irish Times*, 8 December.

Boland, John (2001), Review of *That they May Face the Rising Sun*. *Irish Independent*, 8 December.

Bonafous-Murat, Carole (1994), "Le rivage et la terre: l'espace féminin dans *Amongst Women*", eds. Jean Brihault et Liliane Louvel, *La Licorne (numéro spécial John McGahern)*, Poitiers: 137–50.

Bradfield, Scott (1992), Review of *The Collected Stories*, *Independent* (London), 17 October.

Brihault, Jean et Liliane Louvel (eds.) (1995), *La Licorne, Numéro Spécial John McGahern*, Poitiers: UFR Langues Littératures. October.

Broderick, John (1975), "Memory and Desire", (review of *The Leavetaking*), *Hibernia*, 39 (1).

Brown, Terence (1979), "John McGahern's *Nightlines*: Tone, Technique and Symbolism", *The Irish Short Story*, eds. Patrick Rafroidi and Terence Brown, Gerrards Cross: Smythe, 289–301.

Brown, Terence (1991), "Redeeming the Time: The Novels of John McGahern and John Banville", *The British and Irish Novel since 1960*, ed. James Achesan, New York: St. Martin's.

Brown, Terence (1992), "An Imagined Audience", (review of *The Collected Stories*), *Sunday Tribune*, 11 October.

Burgess, Anthony (1963), Review of *The Barracks*, *Observer* (London), 9 March.

Cahalan, James M. (1988), *The Irish Novel: A Critical History*. (Ch. 10: "The Conscience of the Midlands: John McGahern"), Dublin: Gill and Macmillan, 271–5.

Cahalan, James M. (1995), "Female and Male Perspectives on Growing Up Irish in Edna O'Brien, John McGahern and Brian Moore", *Colby Quarterly*, 31 (March), 55–73.

Cahalan, James M. (1999), *Double Visions: Women and Men in Modern and Contemporary Irish Fiction*, Syracuse, NY: Syracuse University Press.

Cardin, Bertrand (1994), "L'Incommunicabilité dans *The Barracks*", *Études Irlandaises*, Numéro Spécial (Octobre), 65–74.

Chevalier, Jean-Louis (1996), "Childhood in *The Barracks*", *Études Irlandaises*, 21 (Automne), 171–81.

Cleary, Joe (2000), "Modernization and Aesthetic Ideology in Contemporary Irish Culture", *Writing in the Irish Republic: Literature, Culture, Politics 1949–1999*, ed. Ray Ryan, London: Macmillan, 105–29.

Coad, David (1994), "Religious References in *The Barracks*", *Études Irlandaises*, Numéro Spécial (Octobre), 131–8.

Coad, David (1995), "One God, One Disciple: the Case of John McGahern", *Études Britanniques Contemporaines* (Université de Paul Valéry), Janvier, 57–62.

Colgan, Gerry (1991), "Sadly Risible Drama Debut for McGahern" (review of *The Power of Darkness*), *The Irish Times*, 18 October.

Conarroe, Joel (1987), "Strong Women, Dreamy Men" (review of *High Ground*), *New York Times Book Review*, 8 February, 9.

Cooper, Rands Richards (1990), "Goodbye Again, Dark Love" (review of *Amongst Women*), *New York Times Book Review*, 9 September, 44.

Cotter, D. (1982), "Irish Novels of the Developing Self, 1760–1965", PhD, University College, Dublin.

Coyne, Sarah Teresa (1998), "A Study of John McGahern's Novels: The Evolution of the Protagonists in a Repressive Society", PhD, Duquesne University 1995, Ann Arbor, Mich.: UMI Dissertation Services.

Craig, Patricia (1980), "Concocting Erotica" (review of *The Pornographer*), *TLS*, 76.

Craig, Patricia (1985), "Everyday Ecstasies" (review of *High Ground*), *TLS*, 1001.

Cronin, John (1969), "*The Dark* is not Light Enough: The Fiction of John McGahern", *Studies: An Irish Quarterly*, 58 (Winter), 427–32.

Cronin, John (1985), Review of *High Ground*, *Studies: An Irish Quarterly*, 75 (298), 219–21.

Cronin, John (1988), "Art and the Failure of Love: The Fiction of John McGahern", *Studies: An Irish Quarterly*, 77 (Summer),, 201–17.

Cronin, John (1992), "John McGahern's *Amongst Women*: Retrenchment and Renewal", *Irish University Review*, 22 (Spring / Summer), 168–76.

Cronin, John (1994), "'The Frightful Mill of Love': John McGahern's *The Barracks*", *Études Irlandaises*, Numéro Spécial (Octobre), 107–18.

Cronin, John (1996), "John McGahern: A New Image?" *Irish Writers and their Creative Process*, ed. Jacqueline Genet and Wynne Hellegouarc'h, Gerrards Cross: Colin Smythe, 110–17.

Crowley, Cornelius (1995), "Leavetaking and Homecoming in the Writing of John McGahern", *Études Britanniques Contemporaines* (Université de Paul Valéry), Janvier, 63–75.

Dawson, Kevin (1990), "Master of Solitude" (Profile), *The Sunday Tribune*, 9 September, 16.

Deane, Seamus (1986), *A Short History of Irish Literature*, London: Hutchinson.

Deane, Seamus (1990), "A Millimetre Away from Perfection" (review of *Amongst Women*), *Sunday Tribune*, 6 May.

Deane, Seamus (2002), "A New Dawn" (review of *That They May Face the Rising Sun*), *Guardian*, 12 January.

Devine, Paul (1979), "Style and Structure in *The Dark*", *Critique: Studies in Modern Fiction*, 21 (Spring), 49–58.

DiBattista, Maria (1998), "Joyce's Ghost: The Bogey of Realism in John McGahern's *Amongst Women*", *Transcultural Joyce*, ed. Karen R. Lawrence, Cambridge: Cambridge University Press, 21–36.

Donnelly, Peter (1979), Review of *The Pornographer*, *Sunday Press*, 17 October, 14.

Dubois, Dominique (2000), "Incommunicability and Alienation in John McGahern's 'My Love, My Umbrella': An Analysis of the Discursive Strategies", *Journal of the Short Story in English*, 34 (Spring), 53–64.

Duguid, Lindsay (1990), "The Passing of the Old Ways" (review of *Amongst Women*), *TLS*, 18–24 May, 535.

Duperray, Max (1994), "La Pesanteur et la Grâce ou la Passion d'Elizabeth dans *The Barracks*", *Études Irlandaises*, Numéro Spécial (Octobre), 139–46.

Fallis, Richard (1978), *The Irish Renaissance: An Introduction to Anglo-Irish Literature*, Dublin: Gill and Macmillan.

Farren, Ronan (1985), "The Forlorn Fifties" (review of *High Ground*), *Sunday Independent*, 8 September, 14.

Farren, Ronan (1990), "Darkest Leitrim" (review of *Amongst Women*), *Sunday Independent*, 13 May, 28.

Fierobe, Claude (1994), "John McGahern: Le fugitif et l'éternel", *Études Irlandaises*, Numéro Spécial (Octobre), 11–14.

Foley, Michael (1968), "The Novels of John McGahern", *The Honest Ulsterman*, 5 (September), 34–7.

Fournier, S.J. (1987), "Structure and Theme in *The Pornographer*", *Éire-Ireland*, 22 (Spring), 139–50.

Fowles, John (1978), "Irish Keys" (review of *Getting Through*), *Irish Press*, 15 June, 6.

Freyer, Grattan (1983), "Change Naturally: The Fiction of O'Flaherty, O'Faoláin, McGahern", *Éire-Ireland*, 18 (Spring), 138–44.

Fuller, Roy (1970), Review of *Nightlines*, *The Listener*, 26 November, 752.

Ganteau, Jean-Michel (1995), "John McGahern's *The Barracks*: An Interpenetrative Catholic Novel", *Études Britanniques Contemporaines* (Université de Paul Valéry), Janvier, 25–40.

Garcier, Fabienne (1985), "Configurations et Défigurations de l'espace dans les Nouvelles de Mary Lavin, Frank O'Connor et John McGahern", *Cahiers du Centre d'Études Irlandaises*, 3 (January), 54–71.

Garfitt, Roger (1975a), "Silent Traveller" (review of *The Leave-taking*), *The New Review*, February, 63–5.

Garfitt, Roger (1975b), "Constants in Contemporary Irish Fiction", *Two Decades of Irish Writing: A Critical Survey*, ed. Douglas Dunn, Chester Springs, Penn.: Dufour, 207–43.

Gitzen, Julian (1991), "Wheels along the Shannon: The Fiction of John McGahern", *The Journal of Irish Literature*, 1 September.

Glendinning, Victoria (1990), "Original Irish Moran" (review of *Amongst Women*), *Literary Review* (London), May, 10.

Goarzin, Anne (2002), *John McGahern: Reflets d'Irlande*, Rennes: Presses Universitaires de Rennes.

Gorman, Michael (1987), "Unflinching Fidelity: The Work of John McGahern", *Krino*, no. 4 (Autumn), 8–15.

Graham, Colin (1991), "McGahern, John", *Contemporary Novelists*, ed. Lesley Henderson, 5th ed., London: St. James Press, 623–4.

Grene, Nicholas (1992), "John McGahern's *The Power of Darkness*", *Krino*, no. 13, 52–60.

Grennan, Eamon (1995), "John McGahern: Vision and Revisionism", *Colby Quarterly*, 31 (March), 30–9.

Harmon, Maurice (1975), Review of *The Leavetaking*, *Irish University Review*, 5 (Autumn).

Harmon, Maurice (1976), "Generations Apart: 1925–1975", *The Irish Novel in Our Time*, eds. Maurice Harmon and Patrick Rafroidi, Villeneuve-d'Ascq: Publications de l'Université de Lille.

Hegarty, Shane (2003), "Reading the Public", *The Irish Times Weekend Review*, 18 October, 11

Heron, Liz (1985), Review of *High Ground*, *New Statesman*, 13 September.

Hillan King, Sophia (1990), "'Quiet Desperation': Variations on a Theme in the Writings of Daniel Corkery, Michael McLaverty and John McGahern", *Aspects of Irish Studies*, eds. Myrtle Hill and Sarah Barber, Belfast: Institute of Irish Studies.

Holland, Siobhán (1998), "Tact and Tactics: A Case for Matrifocality in John McGahern's *Amongst Women*", *Irish Encounters: Poetry, Politics and Prose since 1880*, ed. Alan Marshall and Neil Sammells, Bath: Sulis, 115–26.

Holland, Siobhán (2000), "Re-Citing the Rosary: Women, Catholicism and Agency in Brian Moore's *Cold Heaven* and John McGahern's *Amongst Women*", *Contemporary Irish Fiction: Themes, Tropes, Theories*, ed. Liam Harte and Michael Parker, London: Macmillan.

Imhof, Rüdiger (2002), *The Modern Irish Novel: Irish Novelists after 1945*, Dublin: Wolfhound, 213–36.

Jamal, Zahir (1978), Review of *Getting Through*, *New Statesman*, 16 June, 822.

Jebb, Julian (1975), "The Call of the Deep" (review of *The Leavetaking*), *TLS*, 10 January, 29.

Jones, David Pryce (1971), Review of *Nightlines*, *New York Times Book Review*, 7 February, 30.

Jordan, John (1985), "The Short Story After the Second World War", *The Genius of Irish Prose*, ed. Augustine Martin, Cork: Mercier, 131–44.

Jordan, Neil (1978), Review of *Getting Through*, *The Irish Times*, 16 June, 10.

Imhof, Rüdiger (2002), *The Modern Irish Novel: Irish Novelists after 1945*, Dublin: Wolfhound Press, 213–36.

Kamm, Jurgen (1990), "John McGahern" *Contemporary Irish Novelists*, ed. Rüdiger Imhof, Tubingen: Gunter Narr Verlag, 175–91.

Keane, Madeleine (1991), "Power Cut." [Review of *The Power of Darkness*.] *Sunday Independent*, 20 October.

Kearney, Richard (1982), "A Crisis of Imagination: An Analysis of a Counter Tradition in the Irish Novel", *Crane Bag Book of Irish Studies*, Eds. Mark Patrick Hederman and Richard Kearney, Dublin: Blackwater, 390–402.

Kemp, Peter (1990), Review of *Amongst Women*, *The Sunday Times*, 6 May.

Kennedy, Eileen (1983), "The Novels of John McGahern: The Road Away Becomes the Road Back", *Contemporary Irish Writing*, eds. James D. Brophy and Richard J. Porter, Boston: Iona College Press / Twayne, 115–26.

Kennedy, Eileen (1989), "Sons and Fathers in John McGahern's Short Stories", *New Irish Writing*, eds. James D. Brophy and Eamon Grennan, Boston: Iona College Press / Twayne, 65–74.

Killeen, Terence (1991), "Versions of Exile: A Reading of *The Leavetaking*", *Canadian Journal of Irish Studies*, 17 (July), 69–78.

Kilroy, Thomas (1985), "The Autobiographical Novel", *The Genius of Irish Prose*, ed. Augustine Martin, Cork: Mercier, 67–75.

Lanters, José (1994), "'It Fills Many a Vacuum': Food and Hunger in the Early Novels of John McGahern", *Canadian Journal of Irish Studies*, 20 (July), 30–40.

Lawrence, Vincent (1990), "No Proud Heroes in Tales of Ireland's Troubles", (review of *Amongst Women*), *Sunday Press*, Living supplement, 29 April, 10.

Lawrence, Vincent (1992), Review of *The Collected Stories*, *Sunday Press*, 29 November, 41.

Lee, Hermione (1992), "Good Manners of the Mind" (review of *The Collected Stories*), *Irish Times*, 17 October.

Lloyd, Richard Burr (1987), "The Symbolic Mass: Thematic Resolution in the Irish Novels of John McGahern", *Emporia State Research Studies*, 36 (Fall), 5–23.

Lloyd, Richard Burr (1989), "Memory Becoming Imagination: The Novels of John McGahern", *Journal of Irish Literature*, 18 (3), 39–44.

Lodge, David (1963), Review of *The Barracks*, *The Spectator*, 8 March, 299.

Louvel, Liliane (1996), "John McGahern: 'Like All Other Men' ou 'La Vanité et la Poursuite du Vent'", *Études Irlandaises*, 21 (Automne), 151–62.

Louvel, Liliane (2000), "'The Writer's Field: Patrols of the Imagi-nation': John McGahern's Short Stories", *Journal of the Short Story in English*, 34, Anger: Presses Universitaires d'Angers (Spring), 65–88.

MacAnna, Ferdia (1985), Review of *High Ground*, *Sunday Independent*, 15 September, 14.

Maher, Eamon (2000), *Crosscurrents and Confluences: Echoes of Religion in Twentieth Century Fiction*. Dublin: Veritas, 139-154.

Maher, Eamon (2001a), "Disintegration and Despair in the Early Fiction of John McGahern", *Studies: An Irish Quarterly*, 90 (357), Spring, 84–91.

Maher, Eamon (2001b), "A Glimpse of Irish Catholicism in John McGahern's *Amongst Women*", *Doctrine & Life*, 51(6) (July/August), 346–55.

Maher, Eamon and Kiberd, Declan (2002), "John McGahern: Writer, Stylist, Seeker of a Lost World", tapescript of October 2001 interview between Eamon Maher and Declan Kiberd, *Doctrine & Life*, 52 (2) (February), 82–97.

Maher, Eamon (2002), Review of *That They May Face the Rising Sun*, *ILS* (Fall).

Maher, Eamon (2003a), "Spirituality in John McGahern's *That They May Face the Rising Sun*", *Reality*, 68, 2 (February), 26–8.

Maher, Eamon (2003b), "Catholicism in the Writings of John McGahern", *Engaging Modernity: Readings of Irish Politics, Culture and Literature at the Turn of the Century*, eds. Michael Böss and Eamon Maher, Dublin: Veritas, 9–28.

Maher, Eamon (2003c), "The Role of Tradition in Contemporary Ireland", *The Irish Times*, 9 June.

Maher, Eamon (2003d), "Circles and Circularity in the Writings of John McGahern", *Nordic Irish Studies* (Autumn/Winter).

Marshall, Oliver (1990), Review of *Amongst Women*, *Studies: An Irish Quarterly*, 79 (Autumn), 332–4.

Mayne, Richard (1966), Review of *The Dark*, *New Statesman*, 18 March, 390.

Mays, Marianne (Koenig) (1991), "'Ravished and Exasperated': The Evolution of John McGahern's Plain Style", *Canadian Journal of Irish Studies*, 17 (July), 38–52.

McHugh, Roger and Maurice Harmon (eds.) (1982), *A Short History of Anglo-Irish Literature from its Origins to the Present Day*, Dublin: Wolfhound.

McMahon, Sean (1968), "The Priest in Recent Irish Fiction", *Éire-Ireland*, 3 (Summer), 105–114.

Mercier, Vivian (1966), "Growing Up in Ireland" (review of *The Dark*), *New York Times Book Review*, 6 March, 50.

Mikowsky, Sylvie (1994), "L'Experience Fictive du Temps dans *The Barracks*", *Études Irlandaises*, Numéro Spécial (Octobre), 147–64.

Molloy, F.C. (1977), "The Novels of John McGahern", *Critique: Studies in Modern Fiction*, 19(1), 5–28.

Molloy, F.C. (1978), "Themes and Techniques in the Contemporary Novel in Ireland", PhD, University College, Dublin.

Montague, John (1976), "John McGahern", *Contemporary Novelists*, 2nd ed., ed. James Vinson, London: St. James Press, 936.

O'Brien, Darcy (1987), "The Real Ireland" (review of *High Ground*), *ILS*, Fall, 31–2.

O'Brien, George (1987), "The Pornographer", *Masterplots: British and Commonwealth Fiction*, Pasadena, California: Salem Press, 1330–4.

O'Brien, Kate (1963), Review of *The Barracks*, *University Review*, 3, No. 4, 59–60.

O'Brien, Veronica (1996), "*The Barracks*: What to Put Next", *Études Irlandaises*, 21 (Automne), 163–70.

O'Dwyer, Riana (1994), "Gender Roles in *The Barracks*", *Études Irlandaises*, Numéro Spécial (Octobre), 147–64.

O'Connell, Shaun (1984), "Door into the Light: John McGahern's Ireland", *Massachusetts Review*, 25 (Summer), 255–68.

O'Faoláin, Nuala (1978), "Worlds Apart" (review of *Getting Through*), *Hibernia*, 6 July.

Ollier, Nicole (1994), "L'Evitement du Sens dans *The Barracks*", *Études Irlandaises*, Numéro Spécial (Octobre), 75–94.

O'Toole, Fintan (1988), "Island of Saints and Silicon: Literature and Social Change in Contemporary Ireland", *Cultural Contexts and Literary Idioms in Contemporary Irish Literature*, ed. Michael Kenneally, Gerrards Cross: Colin Smythe, 11–35.

O'Toole, Fintan (1990), "Both Completely Irish and Universal", (review of *Amongst Women*), *Irish Times*, 15 September.

Owens, Coilín (1980), "McGahern, John", *The Macmillan Dictionary of Irish Literature*, ed. Robert Hogan, London: Macmillan.

Paratte, Henri-D. (1976), "Conflicts in a Changing World: John McGahern", *The Irish Novel in Our Time*, eds. Patrick Rafroidi and Maurice Harmon, Lille: Publications de l' Université de Lille, 311–27.

Paulin, Tom (1978), Review of *Getting Through*, *Encounter*, 50 (June), 70.

Paulin, Tom (1980), Review of *The Pornographer*, *Encounter*, 52 (January), 60–1.

Pelletier, Martine (1994), "Aliénation Individuelle et Crise Identitaire Collective dans *The Barracks*", *Études Irlandaises*, Numéro Spécial (Octobre), 15–26.

Prescott, Peter (1971), Review of *Nightlines*, *Newsweek*, 8 February, 91–2.

Prescott, Peter (1975), "Super-Soap" (review of *The Leavetaking*) *Newsweek*, 17 February, 48.

Quinn, Antoinette (1989), "Varieties of Disenchantment: Narrative Techniques in John McGahern's Short Stories", *Journal of the Short Story in English*, 13 (Autumn), 77–89.

Quinn, Antoinette (1991), "A Prayer for My Daughters: Patriarchy in *Amongst Women*", *Canadian Journal of Irish Studies*, 17 (July), 79–90.

Raban, Jonathan (1975), "Exiles" (review of *The Leavetaking*), *Encounter*, 44 (June), 77–82.

Rogers, Lori (1997), *Feminine Nation: Performance, Gender and Resistance in the Works of John McGahern and Neil Jordan*, Lanham, MD: University Press of America.

Ross, Ciarán (1994), "Some Painful Thoughts About *The Barracks*", *Études Irlandaises*, Numéro Spécial (Octobre), 119–30.

Rushe, Desmond (1991), "No Good Points in the Murk" (review of *The Power of Darkness*), *Irish Independent*, 18 October, 6.

Sampson, Denis (1976), "A Note on John McGahern's *The Leavetaking*", *Canadian Journal of Irish Studies*, 2 (December), 61–5.

Sampson, Denis (1985), Review of *The Leavetaking*, *ILS*, Spring, 43–4.

Sampson, Denis (1985), Review of *High Ground*, *Canadian Journal of Irish Studies*, 13 (2), 61–5.

Sampson, Denis (1991a), "Introducing John McGahern", *Canadian Journal of Irish Studies*, 17 (July), 1–11.

Sampson, Denis (1991b), "The Lost Image: Some Notes on John McGahern and Proust", *Canadian Journal of Irish Studies*, 17 (July), 57–68.

Sampson, Denis (1991c), "John McGahern: A Preliminary Check-list", *Canadian Journal of Irish Studies*, 17 (July), 93–101.

Sampson, Denis (1991d), "John McGahern: Biographical Out-line", *Canadian Journal of Irish Studies*, 17 (July), 91–2.

Sampson, Denis (1992), "The Common Condition" (review of *The Power of Darkness*), *ILS*, 11 (Fall), 11–12.

Sampson, Denis (1993), *Outstaring Nature's Eye: The Fiction of John McGahern*, Washington: Catholic University of America Press.

Sampson, Denis and Dolores MacKenna (1993), "Two Views: The 'Rich Whole' of the Artist" (review of *The Collected Stories*), *ILS*, 12(2), 11–12.

Sampson, Denis (2000), "'The Rich Whole': John McGahern's *Collected Stories* as Autobiography", *Journal of the Short Story in English*, 34 (Spring), 21–30.

Schwartz, Karlheinz (1984), "John McGahern's Point of View", *Éire-Ireland*, 19 (Fall), 92–110.

Sealy, Douglas (1979), "A Moral Tale" (review of *The Pornographer*), *Hibernia*, 25 October, 13.

Sheehy Skeffington, Owen (1966), "The McGahern Affair", *Censorship*, 2 (Spring), 27–30.

Thwaite, Anthony (1975), Review of *The Leavetaking*, *Observer* (London), 5 January, 13.

Tóibín, Colm (1990), "Ritual and Report" (review of *Amongst Women*), *Irish Review*, Autumn, 119–23.

Tóibín, Colm (1992), "McGahern's Treasure House" (review of *The Collected Stories*), *Sunday Independent*, 20 December, 10L.

Toolan, Michael J. (1981), "John McGahern: The Historian and the Pornographer", *Canadian Journal of Irish Studies*, 7 (December), 39–55.

Tosser, Yvon (1979), "Théorie de l'Image, sensibilité absurde et aspects de la pratique textuelle dans *Nightlines*", *Cahiers du Centre d'Etudes Irlandaises*, 4, 7–31.

Tosser, Yvon (1994), "Répétition et différence: l'invention du quotidien dans *The Barracks*", *Études Irlandaises*, Numéro Spécial (Octobre), 95–106.

Updike, John (1979), "An Old-Fashioned Novel" (review of *The Pornographer*), *New Yorker*, 24 December, 95–8. Reprinted in John Updike, *Hugging the Shore: Essays and Criticism*, New York: Knopf, 1983, 388–93.

Verley, Claudine (1996), "Variations sur un incipit: le train et la roue ou 'La forme de l'histoire' dans 'Wheels' de John McGahern", *Études Irlandaises*, 21 (Automne), 137–50.

Vivante, Paulo (1991), "McGahern and the Homeric Moment", *Canadian Journal of Irish Studies*, 7 (July), 53–6.

Wall, Eamonn (1994), *Brian Moore, John McGahern, Aidan Higgins: An Introduction to the New Irish Fiction*, PhD, University of New York, 1992, Ann Arbor: UMI Dissertation Services.

Wall, Eamonn (1999), "The Living Stream: John McGahern's *Amongst Women* and Irish Writing in the 1990s", *Studies: An Irish Quarterly*, 88, 351 (Autumn), 305–14.

Warner, Alan (1978), *A Guide to Anglo-Irish Literature*, Dublin: Gill and Macmillan.

White, Terence de Vere (1965), "Five to One" (review of *The Dark*), *Irish Times*, 8 May, 8.

White, Terence de Vere (1974), "The Sack Race" (review of *The Leavetaking*), *Irish Times*, 4 January.

White, Terence de Vere (1985), "The Conscious Artist" (review of *High Ground*), *Irish Times*, 14 September, 11.

Whyte, James (2002), *Strategies of Transcendence: History, Myth and Ritual in the Fiction of John McGahern*, New York: Edwin Mellen Press.

Wondrich, Roberta Gefter (2000), "Exilic Returns: Self and History Outside Ireland in Recent Irish Fiction", *Irish University Review*, Special Issue: Contemporary Irish Fiction (Spring-Summer), 1–16.

Other Works Consulted

Beckett, Samuel (1970), *Proust*, London: Calder and Boyars.

Booth, Wayne (1961), *The Rhetoric of Fiction*, Chicago: University of Chicago Press.

Brown, Terence (1981), *Ireland: A Social and Cultural History 1922–79*, London: Fontana.

Carlson, Julia (1990), *Banned in Ireland: Censorship and the Irish Writer*, London: Routledge.

Camus, Albert (1989), *The Stranger*, Translation by Matthew Ward, New York: Vintage.

Cronin, John (1992), *Irish Fiction, 1900–1940*, Belfast: Appletree.

Cronin, Michael, Luke Gibbons, Peadar Kirby (eds.) (2002), *Reinventing Ireland: Culture, Society and the Global Economy*, London: Pluto.

Eagleton, Terry (1990), *The Ideology of the Aesthetic*, Oxford: Basil Blackwell.

Fallon, Brian (1998), *An Age of Innocence: Irish Culture 1930-1960*, Dublin: Gill and Macmillan.

Hillan King, Sophia (ed.) (1989), *In Quiet Places: The Uncollected Stories, Letters and Critical Prose of Michael McLaverty*, Dublin: Poolbeg. (Contains a number of letters from Michael McLaverty to John McGahern.)

Hunt Mahony, Christina (1998), *Contemporary Irish Literature: Transforming Tradition*, New York: St Martin's Press.

Joyce, James (1996), *Dubliners*, London: Penguin Popular Classics.

Kenny, Mary (2000), *Goodbye to Catholic Ireland*, Dublin: New Island.

Kiberd, Declan (1995), *Inventing Ireland: The Literature of the Modern Nation*, London: Jonathan Cape.

Kiberd, Declan (2000), *Irish Classics*, London: Granta Books.

Kiberd, Declan (2003), "The Novel and the Story", *The Irish Times Weekend Review*, September 27, 7.

Lee, J.J. (1989), *Ireland 1912–1985: Politics and Society*, Cambridge: Cambridge University Press.

Martin, Augustine (1965), "Inherited Dissent: The Dilemma of the Irish Writer", *Studies: An Irish Quarterly* (Spring), 1–20.

O'Croimhthain, Tomás (1937), *The Islandman*, Trans. Robin Flower. Reprinted Oxford: Oxford University Press, 1978.

O'Malley, Ernie (1936), *On Another Man's Wound*, Reprinted Dublin: Anvil, 1979.

Index